Choosing
the
News

**Recent Titles in Contributions to the
Study of Mass Media and Communications**

CHOOSING THE NEWS

The Profit Factor in News Selection

PHILIP GAUNT

CONTRIBUTIONS TO THE STUDY OF MASS MEDIA
AND COMMUNICATIONS, NUMBER 16
Bernard K. Johnpoll, *Series Editor*

GREENWOOD PRESS
New York • Westport, Connecticut • London

Library of Congress Cataloging-in-Publication Data

Gaunt, Philip.
 Choosing the news.

 (Contributions to the study of mass media and communi-
cations, ISSN 0732–4456 ; no. 16)
 Includes bibliographical references.
 1. Foreign news. 2. Journalism—Economic aspects—
United States. 3. Journalism—Economic aspects—Great
Britain. 4. Journalism—Economic aspects—France.
5. Journalism—Objectivity. 6. Communication—Inter-
national cooperation. I. Title. II. Series.
PN4784.F6G38 1990 070.4'332 89–23466
ISBN 0–313–26847–9 (lib. bdg. : alk. paper)

British Library Cataloguing in Publication Data is available.

Library of Congress Catalog Card Number: 89–23466
ISBN: 0–313–26847–9
ISSN: 0732–4456

First published in 1990

Greenwood Press, Inc.
88 Post Road West, Westport, Connecticut 06881

Printed in the United States of America

The paper used in this book complies with the
Permanent Paper Standard issued by the National
Information Standards Organization (Z39.48–1984).

10 9 8 7 6 5 4 3 2 1

For Jean, who has taught me
that it is never too late

CONTENTS

TABLES

PREFACE AND ACKNOWLEDGMENTS

The idea for this book first came to me several years ago when I was working as a media specialist at UNESCO in Paris. Frequent contact with journalists from all parts of the world led me to wonder about how and why news is selected and whether differences occur from one country to another. Preliminary investigation indicated that there might be some strong similarities, but it soon became obvious that the research required to provide any really satisfactory answers would be far more extensive than anything I could undertake with a busy professional schedule. After more than twenty years in the communications business, I returned to graduate school to complete a Ph.D. Work done at that time provides the basis of this book.

I would like to thank all those journalists who, during the course of my research, allowed me to poke around inside their thought processes, almost always when they were frantically busy and pressed for time. I am grateful, too, to those newspaper editors who allowed me, first, to invade their territory and, second, to inundate them with endless questions. Among them, I am particularly grateful to Michel Poinot of *Le Courier de l'Ouest*, Stuart Garner of the *Eastern Daily Press* and Paul McAuliffe of the Evansville *Courier*. Their knowledge of the newspaper industry in their respective countries has been an inestimable source of information.

I also wish to thank Professors Bonnie Brownlee, Norman Furniss, Owen Johnson and David Weaver, whose suggestions and comments on early drafts have contributed greatly to this book. My thanks, too, to Professor Bernard Johnpoll, who is editor of the series Contributions to the Study of Mass Media and Communications, and whose initial review of the manuscript suggested ways of widening its perspective. In more general terms I feel particularly indebted to David Weaver, whose advice, encouragement and friendship over the years have been unfailing.

My thanks are due, too, to the Mellon Foundation and the Indiana University Center for West European Studies for their generous support.

Finally, I want to thank my wife, Jean, whose wisdom and good humor helped me to keep a sense of proportion during the many months of research and writing that went into this book.

Choosing
the
News

PART I

JOURNALISTIC IMAGES

1

INTRODUCTION

It is still not clear why journalists make the choices they do; why they select certain news stories and reject others. And yet, insofar as the information we receive from the media shapes the way in which we view the world, it is important for us to understand this process. It is a complex process, influenced by many factors that may vary considerably from medium to medium, from organization to organization, and from culture to culture. This study looks at a very specific aspect of this process: the selection of foreign news in regional newspapers in France, Great Britain and the United States. Despite its specific focus, however, it also seeks to explain the news selection process as part of an overall image of journalism, shared by individual journalists, news organizations and society as a whole.

The study makes use of systematic content analysis to determine what types and quantities of foreign news are reported in three medium-sized regional newspapers: the *Courier* in Evansville, Indiana; the *Eastern Daily Press* in Norwich, Britain; and the *Courier de l'Ouest* in Angers, France. The analysis covers a period of two weeks, from May 4 to May 15, 1987. Over the same period, an analysis is also made of foreign news coverage in the wire services taken by the newspapers: the AP in the United States, the Press Association in Britain, and Agence France Presse and the French service of the AP in France.

Participant observation has also been used to study newsroom procedures in each of the three newspapers, also over a two-week period. This observation is supplemented by interviews both with journalists working on foreign news, and with senior editorial and management staff. Finally, survey questionnaires give some indication of how journalists rank a number of criteria used in the selection of foreign news. General context is provided by a broad study of the history and traditions of each country's journalistic culture, including journalism training.

The findings of the content analysis, reported in Chapter 6, show that there are in fact very few significant differences in foreign news coverage either in the three newspapers or in the four news agencies examined. In view of the widely divergent journalistic images still prevalent in the three countries, these results may be surprising, and it is tempting to link the few differences that are observed to the continued existence of such images. However, it is obvious that other factors are at work here that are producing such homogeneous results.

As is discussed below, a number of researchers have attempted to explain how media content is affected by professional routines, organizational constraints, personal idiosyncracies or general societal factors. In all probability, news content is shaped by a combination of these and other influences, set within a broader context of journalistic history, customs and traditions, which together make up the image of journalism prevalent in any given culture.

The findings of this study, however, suggest that the tendency toward more homogeneous media content is also the result of technological innovations associated with changing patterns of ownership and increased emphasis on profitability. The introduction of new technology, particularly in the print media, has been hastened by the commercially oriented newspaper groups that have emerged since the 1950s. Electronic news management systems have been viewed as a way to maximize profit in the face of intense competition from other media. Generally increased newsholes, despite temporary cutbacks caused by the 1973 newsprint shortage, and a relative reduction of editorial staff have encouraged a greater dependence on centralized electronic news sources, and this dependence tends to result in greater uniformity of content.

RELATED STUDIES

A thorough review of the mass communication journals and other research literature published over the past ten years[1] reveals no previous work on the specific focus of this study: the comparison of foreign news coverage and news values in regional newspapers in the United States, Great Britain and France. However, there are a number of studies which have some general relevance to the study. These fall into six main categories.

Comparative International Studies of Newspapers

More has been published on comparative media *systems* than on newspapers per se. Studies range from the classic *Four Theories of the Press*[2] to more recent works such as *Agents of Power*[3] and *Global Journalism*.[4] However, a few studies deal specifically with the press, the most recent and comprehensive being Martin Walker's *Powers of the Press*,[5] which compares twelve of the world's influential newspapers. An earlier comparative study of newspapers in the capitalist, socialist and third worlds, by Gerbner and Marvanyi,[6] concludes that foreign news coverage varies from region to region and that there is a close relationship between commercial sponsorship and foreign news coverage: the greater the level of sponsorship, the lower the coverage. Gertrude Joch Robinson challenges this relationship in a comparative study of foreign news values in the Quebec, English Canadian and U.S. press.[7] Robinson identifies a number of factors influencing the selection of foreign news. Environmental factors such as ownership, circulation, technical facilities, foreign correspondents and diplomatic history may affect the *availability* of foreign news. Organizational constraints and professional values determine space allotment, geographic selection and content focus.

International News Coverage

As K. Kyoon Hur points out,[8] there is an important distinction to be made between the volume and direction of international news flow, as described by Hester,[9] and the actual type of information disseminated as a result of the news values and factors codified by Galtung and Ruge.[10] The present study is, of course, more concerned with the latter, international news *coverage*.

Lent[11] and Semmel[12] have both analyzed foreign news coverage in the U.S. media. Dajani and Donohue have examined foreign news in the Arab press.[13] Atwood and Bullion have sought to define "news maps" of the world in a study of the Asian media.[14] Of more specific interest to the present study is Weaver and Wilhoit's analysis of foreign news coverage in two U.S. wire services.[15]

There are, however, very few studies that analyze foreign news coverage in regional or local newspapers. The most relevant is Wilhoit and Weaver's follow-up to their 1981 study: "Foreign News Coverage in Two U.S. Wire Services: An Update,"[16] about which more will be said later. There is also a 1982 M.A. thesis by Gail Smith of the University of Georgia analyzing UPI news flow to seven Georgia daily newspapers.[17] Perhaps the most interesting finding of Smith's study is that newspaper editors overestimated the amount of foreign news in their publications by sizeable margins. Finally, more general background information is provided by such writers as Jeremy Tunstall,[18] Anthony Smith[19] and Rosemary Righter.[20]

A number of studies also appeared in the wake of the UNESCO "free flow" controversy. The Foreign Images study undertaken for UNESCO by the International Association for Mass Communication Research[21] is "essentially concerned with the role played by the media in portraying foreign countries and foreign affairs to the public, and the consequences of this for social consciousness."[22] This study, which examined twenty-nine media systems around the world, concludes that while content may be different, "what does appear to have become almost universal is the selection of the same foci in international news reporting."[23]

Stevenson and Shaw's book, *Foreign News and the New World*

Information Order,[24] is largely a report on the results of the American team that worked on the UNESCO/IAMCR study. The authors determine that many of the complaints about Western coverage of the Third World are not justified, but that foreign news in the Western media is spotty, narrowly defined and uneven. They conclude that the problems of world news flow are less problems of Western dominance than problems of journalism.

The Regional Press in the United States, Britain and France

Once again, there are no specific studies comparing regional newspapers in the three countries, but there are a number of general works that include details about the regional press.

The two most recent and relevant works on the American press are *The Media in America* by John Tebbel,[25] and *American Newspapers in the 1980s* by Ernest Hynds,[26] both of which emphasize the increasing prosperity of local newspapers as well as concentration of ownership.

On the British press, the most recent and comprehensive study is *The Media in Britain* by Jeremy Tunstall,[27] which focuses more particularly on the national and electronic media but which predicts a difficult future for the regional media throughout the rest of the 1980s. Anthony Smith's book, *The British Press Since the War*,[28] deals more specifically with government documents about the press. Denis McQuail's *Analysis of Newspaper Content*[29] deals with both national and local press. Finally, there are three informative works, specifically about the "provincial" press in Britain, by Jackson,[30] Clark,[31] and Simpson.[32] More will be said about these in a later chapter.

There are several good books on the French press as a whole, the most complete and least political being those by Pierre Albert[33] and Emmanuel Derieux.[34] An excellent neo-Marxist analysis is provided by J.W. Freiberg.[35] A recent work by Michel Mathien, *La Presse Quotidienne Régionale*,[36] gives a good up-to-date description of the regional press. Archambault and Lemoîne,[37] both sons of influential editors, paint a somewhat idyllic picture of the French local press, unjustly threatened by the labor unions. Alain Besson,[38] in direct contradiction to these two writers, sees a lot wrong with the French provincial press which, in his opinion, offers a distorted, paternalistic, soothing image of real life in the French provinces.

The Flow of News from Wire Service to Local Newspapers

A great deal has been written about the international news agencies, particularly since the 1970s when the "Big Four"[39] came under heavy attack from the Third World, which accused them of being responsible for an "imbalance" in world news reporting. But the only recent study to deal with the specific topic of news flow from wire service to local newspapers is the previously cited article by Wilhoit and Weaver, "Foreign News Coverage in Two U.S. Wire Services: An Update." This article refutes the claim that the bulk of foreign news is made up of coups and earthquakes as suggested by Mort Rosenblum.[40] Using content analysis, it tracks foreign news from the AP IB wire and the UPI state wire to eleven randomly selected small circulation newspapers in Indiana. The study shows that "with a few significant exceptions, small newspapers used foreign news items in proportion to the numbers of these items received from the wire services." But, the study goes on to state: "The tendency of wire services to give more frequent coverage to news of conflict in developing nations was enhanced by the even greater proportionate use of such dispatches by the newspapers."

These findings are particularly interesting in the light of Third World accusations of "biased reporting," and one of the secondary aims of this book is to see if these findings apply to regional newspapers in other countries. It is therefore a partial replication of the Wilhoit and Weaver study.

Professional Roles and Values of Journalists

While much American mass communication research has focused on media effects, and a lot of European research has been more concerned with media policy and government-media relations, there has been a slowly growing body of work, on both sides of the Atlantic, devoted to the journalist at work. One of the earliest studies of this nature was Warren Breed's "Social Control in the Newsroom."[41] This was followed in 1969 by Gaye Tuchman's work on "News, the Newsman's Reality."[42] Jeremy Tunstall's book, *Journalists at Work*,[43] published in 1971, was the first to apply a sociological framework to the study of specialized correspondents and has since become a classic in its genre.

More recently, researchers like Christian[44] have begun to look at occupational ideologies, while others, like Gans,[45] have investigated news selection criteria in large newsroom settings. A group of researchers in Europe, in particular Schlesinger,[46] Cayrol,[47] and Gurevitch and Blumler,[48] have done major observational studies of television news operations. A systematic study of U.S. journalists, their ethics and professional roles and values, has been undertaken by Gray and Wilhoit[49] and Wilhoit, Weaver and Gray,[50] building on earlier work by Johnstone, Slawski and Bowman.[51]

Theories of News Content

While a great deal of excellent work has been done on the subject of news values, most of the studies completed to date have been undertaken without the unifying influence of a general theory of news content. The result has been a collection of disparate and sometimes conflicting explanations about various isolated parts of the journalistic process. In a recent monograph,[52] Shoemaker and Mayfield have analyzed this body of work, outlining new approaches to theory building. Expanding on the work of Gans[53] and Gitlin,[54] they group studies into five theoretical approaches:

1. Content reflects social reality with little or no distortion.
2. Content is a function of media routines.
3. Content is influenced by journalists' socialization and attitudes.
4. Content results from social and institutional forces acting upon it.
5. Content is a function of ideological positions and a tool of the status quo.

Building on an idea developed by Altschull,[55] Shoemaker and Mayfield seek to integrate the theoretical approaches they review into an economic model that explains media content as the product of a complex set of ideological forces held by those who fund the mass media.

More recently, the present writer has tested some of the "hypotheses" advanced by Shoemaker and Mayfield[56] and has found that they fail to explain a number of factors influencing the journalistic process, in particular the importance of news agencies as agenda setters, the relative strength of labor unions, the diversity of news gathering and processing structures, the size of media vehicles and, above all, the image of media vehicles and those who work for them. It is argued that while Shoemaker and Mayfield's hypotheses account for many important factors, they would have greater explanatory power if they were given the extra contextual dimension of image, which *includes* rather than *negates* the ideology-of-media-financiers idea introduced by Altschull.

THEORETICAL FRAMEWORK AND SIGNIFICANCE OF THE STUDY

The theoretical framework of the study is a simple one, based on observation and a long-standing familiarity with the media systems of the United States, France and Britain. In each of these three countries, perceptions of journalistic roles are manifestly very different, and one might expect news coverage to reflect these differences. However, even a cursory examination of the media in these countries shows that the kinds of news stories selected are in fact very similar. Is this similarity real or only apparent? If it is real, why is there a disparity between journalistic role perceptions and actual journalistic practices? Is this disparity the result of changes that are taking place in journalistic procedures? If so, what are the factors behind these changes?

In answering these questions, this study expands previous research on:

1. Foreign news flow from wire service to local newspapers
2. International news coverage

3. Comparative studies of newspapers
4. Studies of the regional press
5. Professional roles and values of journalists
6. General theories of news content

From the outset, it was postulated that the news selection process is mainly governed by professional and personal values, as researchers such as White, Breed, Tuchman and Gans have found,[57] but that these values are affected by other influences of a structural or environmental nature. It was felt that existing research on news content has tended to view the influences affecting the news selection process as independent factors and that there is a need to develop a system of classification that can show how these various factors interact with each other. Interviews with journalists and lengthy observation periods in newsrooms in France, Britain and the United States have suggested a new taxonomy that is outlined and explicated in Chapter 6.

The study compares the content and editorial procedures of three regional newspapers in France, Britain and the United States. The three countries selected all have different media systems, political institutions, cultural traditions and journalistic images, thus providing a kind of "triangulation" of findings. Furthermore, their newspaper industries are all at different stages of technological development, particularly with regard to electronic news management systems.

Medium-sized newspapers of comparable size from comparable regions have been selected because it is felt that provincial journalists are likely to be less affected by some of the heavy competitive and hierarchical pressures that Philip Schlesinger suggests are present in the national media.[58] Finally, *foreign* news has been taken as an indicator of editorial selection because it is less affected by domestic issues and, therefore, is likely to remain constant across cultures.

RESEARCH METHODS AND VALIDITY

The study makes use of three distinct research methods: content analysis, participant observation and survey. These methods have already been outlined at the beginning of this chapter and will be described in detail in Chapter 5. Even so, it might be worth pointing out here that, while the three research methods are quite distinct, they are also used in conjunction with each other. Independent random sampling has not been used so it has not been possible to apply inferential statistics to the results of the content analysis. However, the context provided by observational study of editorial roles and procedures, by survey questionnaires that rank criteria of news selection, and by a consideration of the national and local frameworks in which each newspaper is situated should lend considerable perspective to the findings.

Taken individually, each of the research methods used raises problems of external validity, mainly because the phenomena being studied are very specific. It is obvious that the content analysis of one regional newspaper in a given country is not going to produce widely representative results. Nor can the observation of a small number of journalists within a single newspaper newsroom produce data applicable to other kinds of journalism in, say, the broadcast media. And, without a large random sample, the survey questionnaires used in the study cannot yield any generalizable findings.

However, although these are genuine problems, the nature of the study is such that too much emphasis should not be placed on them. The study uses comparative methods to identify factors affecting the selection of foreign news, and then proposes a system of classification that makes it possible to understand how these factors interact with each other. Without further empirical testing, external validity will remain limited, but a great deal has been done to maximize internal validity by establishing close equivalences among the phenomena being observed. For example, the newspapers have been carefully selected to make sure that they are similar in relative size, type, structure and readership, while observation concentrates exclusively on journalists engaged in the selection of foreign news. With regard to external validity, observation and interviews have also been extended to other newspapers so as to ascertain that the journalists observed are relatively typical for each country.

OUTLINE OF THE STUDY

This chapter has outlined the scope, focus and significance of the study. Chapter 2 examines journalistic traditions and practices in the United States, Britain and France. It discusses some of the historical reasons why perceptions of journalistic roles differ from culture to culture. It also analyzes the different images of journalism held by the general public, media organizations and individual journalists. How journalists view their own roles may be affected by a number of factors, including training. Chapter 3 compares journalism training in each of the three countries and also describes the social and educational background of French, British and U.S. journalists. Chapter 4 looks at some of the significant changes that have taken place in journalism since the end of World War II, in particular techological innovations and patterns of ownership, which have had a profound effect on news processing. Chapter 4 also describes the regional press in the three countries under study.

Chapter 5 gives a nontechnical overview of how the study was conducted, describing the wire services and newspapers analyzed and explaining why they were selected. It gives a detailed description of newsroom procedures and personnel, and provides a background news profile for the period studied, based on foreign news reported in the *New York Times*, the *Times* of London and *Le Monde*.

Chapter 6 reports the findings of the content analysis, establishing the different proportions between and within the various subject categories in each media vehicle, and comparing wire service to wire service, newspaper to wire service and newspaper to newspaper. It also proposes a taxonomy of factors affecting the selection of foreign news and suggests how these factors interact with each other.

Finally, Chapter 7 discusses the findings of the study, concluding that while different images of journalism may continue to exist for some time in each of the three countries, the uniformity of news selection found may be explained by managerial influences associated with competition and changing patterns of ownership. The profit motive driving modern newspaper management practices is seen to function as an invisible gate-keeper. The chapter speculates whether increasing uniformity of news coverage is inevitable, given the commercial forces at work, or whether alternative forms of media ownership offer the possibility of renewed diversity. In conclusion, the chapter outlines some future research directions suggested by the findings of the study.

Appendix I provides a full-length methodological note discussing context, rationale for the study, research design, validity, generalizability, etc. It also gives a detailed explanation of coding categories and questionnaires. Finally, Appendix II brings together the codes of journalistic conduct published by the National Union of Journalists in Britain, the French Syndicat National des Journalistes and the American Society of Newspaper Editors.

NOTES

1. *Mass Communication Review Yearbook, Communication Yearbook, Journalism Quarterly, Journal of Communication, Critical Studies in Mass Communication, Communication Abstracts, Les Cahiers de la Communication, Journalism Abstracts, Media, Culture and Society, Gazette.*

2. Frederick Siebert, Theodore Peterson and Wilbur Schramm, *Four Theories of the Press* (Urbana: University of Illinois Press, 1956).

3. J. Herbert Altschull, *Agents of Power: The Role of the News Media in Human Affairs* (New York: Longman, 1984).

4. John C. Merrill (ed.), *Global Journalism: A Survey of the World's Mass Media* (New York: Longman, 1983).

5. Martin Walker, *Powers of the Press: Twelve of the World's Influential Newspapers* (New York: Pilgrim Press, 1983).

6. George Gerbner and George Marvanyi, "The Many Worlds of the World's Press," *Journal of Communication* 27:1 (Winter 1977), pp. 52–66.

7. Gertrude J. Robinson, "Foreign News Values in the Quebec, English Canadian and U.S. Press: A Comparison Study," *Canadian Journal of Communication* 9:3 (Summer 1983), pp. 1–32.

8. K. Kyoon Hur, "A Critical Analysis of International News Flow Research," *Critical Studies in Mass Communication* 1 (1984), pp. 365–378.

9. Al Hester, "Theoretical Considerations in Predicting Volume and Direction of International Information Flow,"*Gazette* 19:4 (1973), pp. 239–247.

10. Johan Galtung and Mari H. Ruge, "The Structure of Foreign News," *Journal of Peace Research* 2:1 (1965), pp. 64–91.

11. John A. Lent, "Foreign News in American Media," *Journal of Communication* 27:1 (Winter 1977), pp. 46–51.

12. Andrew K. Semmel, "Foreign News in Four U.S. Elite Dailies: Some Comparisons," *Journalism Quarterly* 53:4 (Winter 1976), pp. 732–736.

13. N. Dajani and J. Donohue, "Foreign News in the Arab Press: A Content Analysis," *Gazette* 19:3 (1973), pp. 154–170.

14. L.E. Atwood and S.J. Bullion, "News Maps of the World: A View from Asia," in L.E. Atwood and S.M. Murphy (eds.), *International Perspectives on the News* (Carbondale: Southern Illinois University Press, 1982).

15. David H. Weaver and G. Cleveland Wilhoit, "Foreign News Coverage in Two U.S. Wire Services," *Journal of Communication* 31:2 (Spring 1981), pp. 55–63.

16. G. Cleveland Wilhoit and David H. Weaver, "Foreign News Coverage in Two U.S. Wire Services: An Update," *Journal of Communication* 33:2 (Spring 1983), pp. 132–148.

17. Gail Smith, "An Analysis of UPI News Flow from Developed and Developing Nations to Seven Georgia Newspapers" (M.A. thesis, University of Georgia, 1982).

18. Jeremy Tunstall, *The Media are American: Anglo-American Media in the World* (London: Constable, 1977).

19. Anthony Smith, *The Geopolitics of Information: How Western Culture Dominates the World* (New York: Oxford University Press, 1980).

20. Rosemary Righter, *Whose News? Politics, the Press and the Third World* (London: Burnett Books, 1978).

21. Annabelle Sreberny-Mohammadi, Kaarle Nordenstreng, Robert Stevenson and Frank Ugboajah (eds.), "Foreign News in the Media: International Reporting in 29 Countries," *Reports and Papers on Mass Communication* No. 93 (Paris: UNESCO, 1985).

22. Letter from James Halloran, President of the International Association for Mass Communication Research (IAMCR), to selected member states of UNESCO, July 26, 1977 as reported in Sreberny-Mohammadi et al., "Foreign News in the Media."

23. Sreberny-Mohammadi et al., "Foreign News in the Media," p. 52.

24. Robert L. Stevenson and Donald L. Shaw (eds.), *Foreign News and the New World Information Order* (Ames: Iowa State University Press, 1984).

25. John Tebbel, *The Media in America* (New York: Thomas Y. Crowell, 1974).

26. Ernest Hynds, *American Newspapers in the 1980s* (New York: Hastings House, 1980).

27. Jeremy Tunstall, *The Media in Britain* (New York: Columbia University Press, 1983).

28. Anthony Smith (ed.), *The British Press since the War* (Newton Abbot: David and Charles, 1974).

29. Denis McQuail, *Analysis of Newspaper Content* (London: HMSO, 1977).

30. Ian Jackson, *The Provincial Press and the Community* (Manchester: Manchester University Press, 1971).

31. Peter Clark, *Sixteen Million Readers: Evening Newspapers in the U.K.* (London: Holt, Rinehart and Winston, 1981).

32. D.H. Simpson, *Commercialization of the Regional Press* (Aldershot: Gower, 1981).

33. Pierre Albert, *La presse française* (Paris: La Documentation Française, 1978).

34. Emmanuel Derieux, *La presse quotidienne française* (Paris: Armand Colin, 1974).

35. J.W. Freiberg, *The French Press: Class, State and Ideology* (New York: Praeger, 1981).

36. Michel Mathien, *La presse quotidienne régionale*, 2d ed. (Paris: P.U.F., 1986).

37. François Archambault and Jean-François Lemoîne, *Quatre milliards de journaux* (Paris: Alain Moreau, 1977).

38. Alain Besson, *La presse locale en liberté surveillée* (Paris: Les Editions Ouvrières, 1977).

39. The Associated Press, United Press International, Reuters and Agence France Presse.

40. Mort Rosenblum, *Coups and Earthquakes: Reporting the World for America* (New York: Harper and Row, 1979).

41. Warren Breed, "Social Control in the Newsroom: A Functional Analysis," *Social Forces* 33 (1955), pp. 325–335.

42. Gaye Tuchman, "News, the Newsman's Reality" (Ph.D. dissertation, Brandeis University, 1969).

43. Jeremy Tunstall, *Journalists at Work: Special Correspondents, Their News Organizations, News Sources and Competitor-Colleagues* (London: Constable, 1971).

44. Harry Christian, "Journalists' Occupational Ideologies and Press Commercialization," in Harry Christian (ed.), *The Sociology of Journalism and the Press*, Monograph 29 (Keele: University of Keele, 1980).

45. Herbert J. Gans, *Deciding What's News: A Study of CBS Evening News, NBC Nightly News, Newsweek and Time* (New York: Vintage Books, 1980).

46. Philip Schlesinger, *Putting Reality Together: BBC News* (London: Constable, 1978).

47. Roland Cayrol, *L'ORTF face aux élections de mars 1973: une étude d'observation du service politique de la première chaîne de télévision française* (Strasbourg: European Political Consortium for Political Research, 1974).

48. Michael Gurevitch and Jay Blumler, "The Construction of Election News: An Observation Study at the BBC," in James S. Ettema and D. Charles Whitney (eds.), *Individuals in Mass Media Organizations* (Beverly Hills, Calif.: Sage, 1982), pp. 179–204.

49. Richard G. Gray and G. Cleveland Wilhoit, "Portrait of the U.S. Journalist, 1982–1983." Presented to the American Society of Newspaper Editors Convention, Denver, Colorado, May 9, 1983.

50. G. Cleveland Wilhoit, David H. Weaver and Richard G. Gray, "Professional Roles, Values and Ethics of Journalists in Three Democratic Societies," presented at the Sociology and Social Psychology Section meetings of the 14th Conference and General Assembly of the International Association for Mass Communication Research, Prague, Czechoslovakia, August 27-September 1, 1984.

51. John W.C. Johnstone, Edward J. Slawski and William D. Bowman, "The Professional Values of American Newsmen," *Public Opinion Quarterly* 36:4 (Winter 1972–73), pp. 522–540.

52. Pamela Schoemaker and Elizabeth Mayfield, "Building a Theory of News Content: A Synthesis of Current Approaches," *Journalism Monographs* 103 (June 1987).

53. Gans, *Deciding What's News*, pp. 78–115.

54. Todd Gitlin, *The Whole World is Watching* (Berkeley: University of California Press, 1980), pp. 249–282.

55. Altschull, *Agents of Power*, pp. 254–257.

56. Philip Gaunt, "Image Versus Ideology: A Further Step Toward a Theory of News Content Based on a Comparative Study of French and British Newspapers," presented at the 14th Annual Conference of the Midwest Association for Public Opinion Research, Chicago, November 18–19, 1988.

57. David M. White, "The Gate-Keeper: A Case Study in the Selection of News," *Journalism Quarterly* 27:3 (Fall 1950) pp. 383–396; Breed, "Social Control in the Newsroom"; Tuchman, "News, the Newsman's Reality"; Gans, *Deciding What's News*.

58. Schlesinger, *Putting Reality Together*, p. 107.

2

JOURNALISTIC TRADITIONS

It is not easy to define journalistic images, partly because there is often confusion among the terms *image, function, role* and *perception*, but also because images have shifted considerably over the last few decades as new ownership patterns and increased competition have brought profound changes to the profession. For the purposes of this study, journalistic images are defined as global images, embracing the concepts of role and role perception as they are understood by the public, by organizations and by individual journalists. There is no doubt that these images of journalism are different in France, Britain and the United States, particularly in popular imagination.

Journalistic images are largely the result of journalistic traditions, which are themselves shaped by history. Traditions are created and perpetuated by the laws, economic constraints, political pressures and social dynamics of the culture in which they appear. Given the historical differences that exist among the sociopolitical structures and intellectual preoccupations of France, Britain and the United States, it is not surprising that journalistic roles, and the way in which they are perceived, should be different in each country.

The French tend to think of journalism as a romantic profession practiced by hardened intellectuals, sometimes with strong political opinions. A typical example is the television journalist portrayed by Yves Montand in the film *Un homme et une femme* *(A Man and a Woman)*, a foreign reporter always ready to jump on a plane and head for the latest hot spot, but a man, also, whose radical leanings prompt him to criticize the system that is the cause of so much conflict and suffering.

An American stereotype is provided by Humphrey Bogart's newspaper reporter in *Deadline USA*, a shirt-sleeved hero with typing fingers like meathooks, eager to fight corruption in high places and defend the cause of TRUTH. Similar versions of this steely-eyed character crop up in many other American motion pictures and literary portrayals.

In British literature, Evelyn Waugh's novel *Scoop*[1] paints a satirical portrait of incompetence in the form of the reluctant war correspondent Boot of the *Beast*. It also portrays the London reporter as an unscrupulous newshound in pursuit of a good "story," a distinctive feature of British journalism about which more will be said later. Perhaps the most colorful image of the British journalist is provided by Keith Williams in *The English Newspaper*. Williams describes him as "a roving buccaneer of print whose published words strike daily at the very core of infamy." However he also refers to him as a "newspaper scribbler," a hack whose "sole weapon is the typewriter across the battered keys of which his nail-bitten, nicotine-stained fingers scramble to write him clear of all those dangers to which he is so vulnerably exposed."[2]

Such depictions are, of course, little short of caricatural, but, however improbable they may be in reality, their place in popular culture affects the way in which the public perceives journalism, and public perceptions may indirectly influence journalistic traditions. Journalistic processes generally, however, are more likely to be shaped by the images held by individual journalists and the organizations for which they work. To understand this better, it is necessary to analyze the notion of image on three different levels: systemic, organizational and individual.

JOURNALISTIC IMAGES

The press as a whole has an image of itself that is shaped by history, tradition and public expectations. Historical considerations, such as press laws, political structures, technological innovations, educational reform, revolution, and cultural or linguistic peculiarities may account for the manner in which journalism has developed in any given country. How journalism reacts to such historical phenomena, as well as to ongoing socioeconomic change, creates a body of journalistic traditions that affect the way news is gathered, processed and disseminated. Public expectations of the press are also affected to a certain extent by history and tradition, but, more often than not, the image that the public has of journalism is shaped by stereotypical portrayals in popular literature and films, as well as by what the different media say about themselves and about each other.

Within this general context, different news organizations have different images of themselves and are thought of differently by the public. The management and editors of a particular newspaper may believe the image of their publication to be quality rather than popular, conservative rather than liberal, or prestigious rather than fashionable. As a consequence, they will encourage their journalists to select stories, report events and develop editorial styles that are in keeping with what they think this image to be.

An example of this is afforded by two provincial dailies in Great Britain, the *Yorkshire Post* in Leeds, and the *Eastern Daily Press* in Norwich, both of which claim to be the largest provincial morning newspaper in the country. The *Yorkshire Post*, which has a tradition of investigative reporting, encourages its journalists to seek beyond the mere facts of a story. The *Eastern Daily Press*, which is approximately the same size, has a more placid, get-the-facts-right editorial policy. The two newspapers are the same size, and yet they have very different images of themselves. The *Yorkshire Post* is convinced that it is an "important" newspaper and that its opinions count for something outside of its immediate readership area. Its management maintains that this image is shared by its readers. The *Eastern Daily Press* is more community oriented, more given to boosterism than to controversy, and, according to its readership surveys, that is the image its more parochial readers prefer.

On an individual level, the role and image of the journalist are affected by a number of variables: training, size and type of organization, journalistic traditions, editorial pressures and personal idiosyncracies. How journalists think of themselves—as disseminators, interpreters, investigators or adversaries—will depend upon the society in which they live, the image of the press in general, and the image of the organization in which they work.

In very general terms, interviews conducted for the study show that French journalists regard themselves as commentators and interpreters, bringing the mysteries of the world and its affairs within the grasp of common people. British journalists consider their role to be the investigation and collection of facts, sometimes with a political aim in view. American journalists believe their primary function to be the pursuit and defense of truth as part of the democratic process, a function that is often incorrectly assumed to be constitutional. These are obviously sweeping generalizations, but they also represent archetypal images within which personal idiosyncracies are contained and combined. In each case, the journalist's role is the reflection of a particular journalistic culture shaped over the years by a whole array of events.

HISTORICAL CONSIDERATIONS

It would be inappropriate here to reproduce a complete history of the press in France, Britain and the United States, but it is certainly useful to consider some of the main historical currents that have contributed to the journalistic traditions and images of those countries. To a very large degree, the history of the press in any country reflects the extent to which printers and journalists have succeeded in defeating or evading authoritarian attempts to control the dissemination of information or opinion. Laws guaranteeing press freedoms are therefore important, but more important is the way in which these laws are applied and interpreted. Both the Constitution of the Soviet Union and the First Amendment of the U.S. Constitution protect freedom of expression, and yet the practice of journalism in each of these two countries is manifestly different. The press systems of European countries lie somewhere between what is *perceived* as the total freedom of the United States and the rigid controls of the

Soviet Union and other totalitarian regimes.[3] Such *perceptions* remain strong even if it is obvious to many that U.S. press freedom is relative and that totalitarian controls are softening under the policy of *glasnost*.

THE UNITED STATES

There is little doubt that it is the First Amendment that sets the United States apart from both France and Britain. Until the First Amendment, government efforts to control the press were just as widespread in the United States as they were in Europe. It can be argued that the Alien and Sedition Acts of 1798 and the Sedition Act of 1918 show that, despite the First Amendment, the U.S. government still has the possibility of applying press controls if it so chooses. However, to all intents and purposes, the First Amendment does effectively protect press freedom and freedom of expression in the United States, and these freedoms have only been strengthened by the opinions of the Supreme Court in a number of First Amendment cases.

The fact that the American press chooses to serve a watchdog role is unconnected with First Amendment principles, although the connection is often implied. This modern interpretation of the function of the press probably springs from the notion of the "Fourth Estate" in eighteenth-century England. At that time, the English press was a powerful political force and, in some respects, acted as an intermediary between the Whigs and the Tories. In the American interpretation of this role, the press is part of the political process in that it monitors the workings of government, and exposes abuses of power, corruption and other wrongdoings by elected officials. Although its tradition of political neutrality is relatively recent, the press likes to view itself as an impartial recorder of history. This is a fundamental difference compared with British newspapers, which have never ceased to be politically committed and which see nothing wrong with this state of affairs provided that political affiliations are overt.

Another important notion borrowed from England is that of the free marketplace of ideas as expressed in Milton's *Areopagitica* in 1644: "Let her [truth] and falsehood grapple; who ever knew truth put to the worse, in a free and open encounter?" This eloquent plea for a free press was largely ignored at the time and since then has been generally dismissed by the British press as naïve. Even Milton did not believe that freedom of expression should be extended to everyone, particularly not to the Catholics, and, within a few years of publishing *Areopagitica*, Milton himself became an official censor.[4]

However, the notion was picked up by the American press some hundred years later and was soon adopted as one of the basic tenets of American journalism. Its effect can be traced through to such modern ideas as equal time, the Fairness Doctrine, and even certain aspects of journalistic objectivity, in particular the balanced presentation of all sides of an argument.

Sociologist Michael Schudson argues that journalistic objectivity such as we know it now did not emerge in the United States until the 1930s in the wake of what he calls "the subjectivization of facts" brought about by loss of faith in democracy and the appearance of public relations. What had passed for objectivity before then was nothing more than the application of the scientific method and the principles of logical positivism.[5]

After the Joseph McCarthy affair in the 1950s, when "objectively" reported news proved to be misleading, objectivity became suspect and Schudson believes this led to the appearance of a "critical culture." However, Gaye Tuchman has argued that objectivity is still very much alive as a "strategic ritual" used by newspeople as a defense mechanism.[6] One of the essential features of this ritual is the systematic presentation of different opinions about an issue, a device that can be traced to Milton's "free and open encounter."

Another important notion is that of "social responsibility." First introduced in 1947 by the report of the Hutchins Commission, *A Free and Responsible Press*, social responsibility was later established as one of the basic tenets of modern U.S. journalism in the influential work, *Four Theories of the Press*.[7] Although the concept has been challenged, the term social responsibility has become a symbol for the ideal of a democratic press.[8]

BRITAIN

In the United States, freedom of the press and freedom of expression are protected by the Constitution, the courts and a whole array of deeply entrenched and publicly supported journalistic principles. The same cannot be said of Britain, where not only is there no formal legislation guaranteeing such freedoms, but there is a law specifically restricting the flow of information, the Official Secrets Act, which, according to Moyra Grant, was rushed through Parliament one quiet Friday afternoon in 1911 at the height of a German spy scare.[9] According to Grant, all civil servants, government workers and even teachers are required to sign this act, which covers all official information that is not formally authorized as nonsecret. Grant also claims that there are eighty-nine other acts of Parliament containing secrecy clauses. And then, of course, there is the "D Notice" system, which derives from media censorship during World War II. Under this system, editors are told of certain military secrets and asked voluntarily not to use them.[10]

This having been said, it should also be emphasized, as Jeremy Tunstall has, that "Britain has less legislation specifically about the media than does almost any other country."[11] Tunstall also suggests that the voluntary restraint of the media is far more effective than legislation and compulsion. "The voluntary approach depends of course on consensus, and would only be possible in a nation with a high level of consensus and homogeneity of approach; these of course have long existed—more or less—not least because of the strength of Britain's national media."[12]

Despite legislation, and most of it that affects the media is recent, Britain does have a tradition—only partly mythical—of press freedom and objectivity. From the middle of the sixteenth century until almost the end of the seventeenth century, printing in England was controlled, at one time or another, by the Stationers Company, the Court of Star Chamber and a number of licensing laws. When the Licensing Act was allowed to expire in 1694, prior restraint came to an end.[13] New forms of newspapers began to appear in a heady climate of freedom, observed with a combination of envy and horror by writers and statesmen throughout Europe.[14]

This new climate of freedom, although somewhat restricted by laws of treason and seditious libel, produced a current of political factionalism that has continued to this day. Another current of journalism that began around this time was the impartial reporting of the facts, a procedure much vaunted by Samuel Buckley, the energetic publisher of England's first daily newspaper, the *Daily Courant,* founded in 1702.[15] A third current, still alive today, was the reporting of the morbid, the outrageous and the bizarre. Nathaniel Mist, who ran the successful *Weekly Journal,* was said to have one agent scraping the jails of Middlesex and Surrey for scurrilous crime stories, and another scouring the alehouses and ginshops for drink-related deaths and misdeeds. In 1745, the *Penny London Post* ran a series on hurricanes, earthquakes and volcanoes. And even the celebrated Daniel Defoe, the editor of the *Review,*had been known to stand at the foot of the scaffold to collect the dying words of convicts.[16]

However, despite the cessation of formal licensing, which was politically unviable, it was not long before the government found another means of control, the Stamp Act, first introduced in 1712. The amounts to be paid by newspaper proprietors increased under successive acts until 1836, when they were reduced. These so-called "taxes on knowledge" continued until 1855, and it is no coincidence that the first English penny paper—the *Telegraph*—did not appear until that date. It has been argued that the Stamp Act was kept on in the nineteenth century as a means of inhibiting the development of the radical press,[17] although it could also be argued that the radical press would have failed in any case because of its inability to attract advertising.

Whatever other effects they had, the taxes on knowledge certainly succeeded in dividing the availability and accessibility of information along class lines. Until the penny press emerged in 1855, only the relatively wealthy could afford to buy newspapers with any regularity, and this tended to focus news content on middle- and upper-class interests rather than working-class issues. This division has continued until the present day as a firmly established split between London and the provinces, north and south, industrial and residential, drawled and flattened vowels, and even certain styles of journalism.

FRANCE

As has been pointed out, the sovereigns of Europe watched the development of England's unlicensed newspaper system with great distaste and made certain that their own newspaper industries remained under the thumb of absolutist authority, particularly where "official" domestic news was concerned.[18] The circulation of foreign news was apparently viewed with a more tolerant eye.[19] France favored a heavily controlled and centralized system, and, while there was no lack of diversity of available news forms, they were all subjected to official supervision. Even the public reading of the latest news for the benefit of the illiterate was carefully controlled. However, it should be pointed out that, in the best absolutist traditions, the elaborate licensing system set up and run by Chrétien Malesherbes was intended more to help and enlighten than to repress.[20]

For a very long time, information in France was centralized around three official publications, the *Gazette*, the *Journal des Savants* and the *Mercure*. The *Gazette* was founded by one of the most remarkable figures in the development of French journalism, Théophraste Renaudot, who, as Commissioner-General for the Poor, had set up an "Office of Addresses" in 1629 to encourage the flow of goods and services between the wealthy and the needy.[21] Renaudot soon found that the centralization of information for his printed "classifieds" also attracted a lot of other news. When, in 1631, he was granted the royal and exclusive privilege of printing and selling news and other accounts of events inside and outside the kingdom, he created the *Gazette*, a four-page weekly, which continued to print semiofficial news from the Court and government offices right up until the Revolution.[22] As it developed, the *Gazette* helped shape the future of French news journalism, but it also became noted for its prose style as well as for its news content.[23]

The *Journal des Savants*, founded in 1665 under the patronage of Colbert, was mainly devoted to accounts of books published both in France and abroad, but it was also authorized to report on the Paris parliament and publish university proclamations and academic discourses, as well as news of the arts.[24] The *Journal des Savants* began as a weekly but became a monthly in 1724. It is still in existence to this day and is published under the auspices of the French Academy of Science.

The third official publication, the *Mercure de France*, was founded in 1672, and, although it started life as a gossip sheet (under the name of *Mercure Galant*), it soon became an essentially literary publication. The *Mercure* continued to appear as a monthly until the French Revolution. It enjoyed considerable success and was imitated in other parts of Europe.[25]

As in other countries, attempts were made in France to publish other news sheets, but licensing remained strict and most new ventures were short-lived. The first French daily, the *Journal de Paris*, which did not appear until 1771, had the greatest difficulty in collecting enough information for a daily edition without running into the privileges of other licensed publications.[26] And so, even though other newspapers gradually emerged, most official information was centralized around a handful of licensed publications for more than 150 years, and strong government controls existed right up until the start of the Third Republic in 1870.

A French press law did finally come into being, but not until July 29, 1881, after a long history of alternating authoritarianism and liberalism. Francis Balle suggests that the two main elements of this law—the right to organize a press enterprise, and the respect of the freedom of others—"constitute, for European liberals, necessary conditions for the exercise of freedom of the press."[27] But Pierre Albert argues that the spirit of the law of 1881 is intended more to limit the abuses of freedom than to restrict its applications. In other words, it relies not on a priori controls but on a posteriori sanctions, a principle that is embodied not only in English common law but also in American press legislation, via the late eighteenth-century interpretations of Blackstone's *Commentaries*. However, while this law has continued to safeguard the freedom to publish and to write, it has not always been able to cope with the economic and technical changes taking place in the market.[28]

The French press, then, has been affected by a set of structural differences that do not appear in many other countries. French journalism has always been more a journalism of expression than a journalism of observation, with a marked preference for commentary rather than reporting. It has been concerned with subjective analysis and a critique of intentions rather than a strict recounting of facts, which makes it very different from Anglo-American reporting with its preference for the "objective."

Some aspects of French journalism may be explained partly

by the literary ambitions of French journalists, shared, it should be added, by the journalists of most other countries of continental Europe, both east and west. Another explanation is afforded by the traditionally strong restrictions exercised by the government. Tight control of sources has meant that the French press has often been reduced to criticizing official information rather than hunting down its own news. Even today, because of the breadth and variety of its services, the government controlled Agence France Presse reduces the work of newspapers and supports the tendency to treat news at a secondary level, defining the role of the journalist as one of reflective and critical analysis rather than active news gathering.

JOURNALISTIC ROLES

What emerges from this brief overview of the development of the press in the United States, Britain and France is a set of stereotypical journalistic images that may now be in the process of changing but that are still firmly implanted in the popular imagination. Because of the laws and other historical events that have shaped the growth of journalism in the United States, the American journalist emerges as a watchdog, historian and defender of the truth. As such he is considered to be a vital part of the democratic process. In Britain, press traditions have produced a journalist who is a careful reporter of facts, an imaginative storyteller, and, sometimes, a dedicated champion of political causes. His approach to his profession is that of a craftsman. The French journalist, by contrast, emerges from history as a commentator rather than a reporter, an interpreter of facts, an intellectual and a literary artist.

Like all stereotypes, these images are approximate and overgeneralized, but they have been supported by events in recent history. In the United States, Watergate confirmed the watchdog role of the press, and further strengthened the conviction that the press not only records history but also takes a hand in shaping the destiny of the country. More recently, the outrage of the press over Grenada demonstrated once again its belief that it has the right of access to all information, secret or otherwise, and that it has a duty to make it public in the interests of democracy.

In Britain, the press's treatment of the Profumo affair in the early 1960s showed its predilection for both political activism and voyeurism. It did not let go of the story until Profumo resigned. In the same way, the exposure of Jeffrey Archer's association with a call girl in 1987 caused the well-known writer/politician to resign his position as deputy chairman of the Conservative Party. In each affair, the scandal was used for political purposes, although, of course, it also made for spicy reading. In both cases, the British press, unlike the American press during the Gary Hart affair, was more interested in the scandal than in demonstrating its influence on the democratic process.

France too has had its political scandals. During the last days of the Fourth Republic, the press regaled a delighted public with details of the *ballets roses*, a ring of older and rather well-known members of parliament who sought the favors of adolescent girls. Although a number of reputations were damaged in the process, the French press seemed more interested in commenting upon the inadequacies of a political system that was ready for reform. At the time, both the press and the public were tired of an endless succession of revolving-door governments. The case of Giscard's diamonds, in more recent years, was used more to draw attention to the corruption of public office than to seek the removal of the president. Once again, a scandal was used not to satisfy specific political objectives but to comment upon a general state of affairs, thus reaffirming the journalist's role as interpreter and commentator.

The stereotypical roles that have emerged from history and tradition have changed over the last few decades with the growth of radio and television, with increased commercialization of the media, and with the introduction of modern news gathering and processing procedures that have forced journalists to develop new skills and accept new tasks. Perhaps the greatest change brought by the electronic media is that, now, the journalist is expected to entertain. It could be argued that journalists have always been called upon to entertain, but this aspect of the profession has remained a submerged part of overall role perceptions. What has happened in the past is that "serious" journalism has been associated with certain types of media vehicles, while entertainment has been associated with others. Today, the two may be moving closer together, but the gap between the *New York Times* and the *National Enquirer*, between the *Times* of London and the *Sun*, or between *Le Monde* and *France Dimanche* is unlikely ever to disappear.

It is obvious that entertainment has become an important component of the more popular media. Henry Porter has shown how some London newspapers are not above tampering with photographs or fabricating news,[29] and cites an instance when photographers from the *Daily Star* bought a plastic fried egg from a novelty store so as to illustrate a story about the heat being intense enough to fry an egg on the hood of a car, something they attempted but could not achieve with real eggs. For decades, the French Sunday newspapers have been revealing or predicting rifts, divorce, mysterious illnesses, disasters and other dire happenings in the British royal family. In the United States, the supermarket press has what appears to be an inexhaustible supply of stories about Elvis Presley, aliens from outer space, miraculous births and miracle diets.

This aspect of the press may explain why journalists do not always enjoy the reputation they would like. American journalists have often been criticized for "irresponsible" journalism, misrepresentation, invasion of privacy and harassment. Spiro Agnew's 1969 attack on the press expressed opinions that are shared by many members of the public. In France, the weekly *L'Evénement du Jeudi* ran a recent series of articles under the revealing title: "Salauds de Journalistes?" (Journalist Bastards?).[30] In Britain, public attitudes toward certain segments of the press are summed up by Humbert Wolfe's doggerel:

> You cannot hope to bribe or twist
> (Thank God) the British journalist.
> Considering what the chap will do
> Unbribed, there's no occasion to.[31]

It can be seen from the above that images of journalism are subject to change and may vary from one type of journalism to another. Furthermore, it is becoming axiomatic to say that American journalism, since the 1960s, has been moving toward more interpretive reporting. At the same time, the European media have shown signs of moving toward a more factual style of journalism. In this sense, they are moving closer together; and they are certainly moving closer together on the level of entertainment.

However, despite these subtle changes, the different journalistic images that have emerged from history remain remarkably stable. It is probable that they are perpetuated by a combination of factors that include popular culture, socialization, organizational constraints and training. Of these, journalism training is the strongest formal influence and this is what the next chapter examines.

NOTES

1. Evelyn Waugh, *Scoop* (London: Chapman and Hall, 1938).
2. Keith Williams, *The English Newspaper: An Illustrated History to 1900* (London: Springfield Books, 1977), p. 7.
3. Claude-Jean Bertrand and Miguel Urabayen, "European Mass Media in the 1980s," in Everett Rogers and Francis Balle (eds.), *The Media Revolution in America and Western Europe* (Norwood, N.J.: Ablex, 1985), p. 22.
4. Edwin Emery and Michael Emery, *The Press and America: An Interpretive History of the Mass Media*, 6th ed. (Englewood Cliffs, N.J.: Prentice-Hall, 1988), pp. 11, 682 n.19.
5. Michael Schudson, *Discovering the News: A Social History of American Newspapers* (New York: Basic Books, 1978).
6. Gaye Tuchman, "Objectivity as a Strategic Ritual: An Examination of Newsmen's Notions of Objectivity," *American Journal of Sociology* 77 (January 1972), pp. 660–679.
7. Siebert, Peterson and Schramm, *Four Theories of the Press*.
8. Altschull, *Agents of Power*, pp. 179–205.
9. Moyra Grant, *The British Media* (London: Comedia, 1984), p. 14.
10. Tunstall, *The Media in Britain*, p. 4.
11. Ibid.
12. Ibid.
13. Emery and Emery, *The Press and America*, pp. 8–12.
14. Anthony Smith, *The Newspaper: An International History* (London: Thames and Hudson, 1979), p. 47; Michael Harris and Alan J. Lee (eds.),

The Press in English Society from the Seventeenth to the Nineteenth Centuries (Rutherford, N.J.: Fairleigh Dickinson University Press, 1986).

15. Emery and Emery, *The Press and America*, p. 13.

16. Smith, *The Newspaper*, p. 63.

17. Peter Roger Mountjoy, "The Working Class Press and Working Class Conservatism," in George Boyce, James Curran and Pauline Wingate (eds.), *Newspaper History from the Seventeenth Century to the Present Day* (London: Constable, 1978), pp. 265–280.

18. Smith, *The Newspaper*, p. 47.

19. Jeremy D. Popkin, "The *Gazette de Leyde* and French Politics under Louis XVI," in Jack R. Censer and Jeremy D. Popkin (eds.), *Press and Politics in Pre-Revolutionary France* (Berkeley: University of California Press, 1987), pp. 75–132.

20. Smith, *The Newspaper*, p. 48.

21. Pierre Albert and Fernand Terrou, *Histoire de la presse*, 4th ed. (Paris: P.U.F., 1985), pp. 10–11; Howard M. Solomon, *Public Welfare, Science, and Propaganda in Seventeenth Century France: The Innovations of Théophraste Renaudot* (Princeton, N.J.: Princeton University Press, 1972).

22. Albert and Terrou, *Histoire de la presse*, p. 19.

23. Smith, *The Newspaper*, p. 32.

24. Ibid., p. 51.

25. Albert and Terrou, *Histoire de la presse*, p. 20.

26. Smith, *The Newspaper*, p. 52.

27. Balle, "Communication Revolution and Freedom of Expression," p. 82.

28. Pierre Albert, *La presse française* (Paris: La Documentation Française, 1978), p. 30.

29. Henry Porter, *Lies, Damned Lies and Some Exclusives* (London: Chatto and Windus, 1984), pp. 15–17.

30. *L'Evénement du jeudi*, weeks of February 11–17 and 18–24, 1988.

31. Quoted at the beginning of Henry Porter, *Lies, Damned Lies and Some Exclusives*.

3

JOURNALISM TRAINING

Journalists are an important part of the mass communication process, but, until recent years, relatively little has been written, particularly from a comparative perspective, about the way in which they are trained. In the United States, a great deal of mass communication research, using a behavioral approach, has focused on the impact of media on society. In Europe, research has tended to adopt a more sociological stance in its examination of the relationship between the mass media and power structures. On both sides of the Atlantic, researchers have recognized the pivotal role of journalists in the selection and processing of information fed into the communication process. But, while the question of what causes journalists to make the choices they do has often been asked, no satisfactory answer has ever been given.

It seems obvious that one of the components of an answer, alongside cultural background, professional constraints and newsroom socialization, must be training. In this country, journalism education has frequently come under attack from editors and academics. It is legitimate to wonder whether this is the case in other countries where journalistic habits and practices are different. As in many other areas, a comparative approach to this question may produce some fruitful results.

There has been very little comparative research in journalism training in recent years. In fact, such research is limited to a 1984 study by George Bohère, a couple of UNESCO reports, both published in 1975, and a 1985 article in the *FIEJ Bulletin* giving a brief update of journalism training in eighteen countries.[1] A more recent book by Lee Becker and his colleagues, while mainly concerned with the training and hiring of journalists in the United States, takes a tentative look at journalism education in the Federal Republic of Germany.[2] It also briefly analyzes the impact of the U.S. system on other countries, particularly in the developing countries—an area of research that could be fruitfully expanded.

One of the points most frequently made in this literature is the difference that exists between European and American media training. In the United States, universities have developed to meet social demands and have accepted the responsibility for training, not only in journalism but also in law, engineering, business and other professional areas. In Europe, universities have been viewed traditionally as places for the preservation of culture. As Bertrand and Urabayen have pointed out, "Generally speaking, journalism is not considered a respectable field of university training and research, particularly in such countries as Great Britain and Switzerland."[3]

It is worth pointing out, too, that the system of higher education in Europe is different in many respects from that of the United States. European universities tend to have elitist admission policies often accompanied by rigorous selection processes. In Britain, admission to some universities is still influenced by social background and wealth. In the Federal Republic of Germany, university entrance is heavily dependent upon projected employment requirements. In France, admission to the most prestigious schools is subject to fierce competition.

These systems have their own individual drawbacks and advantages, but they are all based on the same premise: that education should be as broad and nonspecialized as possible. This situation contrasts strongly with that of the United States, where admission to universities is generally democratic, where education tends to become specialized earlier and where educational standards are usually lower than in Europe, at least for undergraduates. Finally, the proportion of young people attending universities in Europe is much lower than in the United States. In 1984, the percentage of the total U.S. population having attended college was 56.2 percent. In the same year, the figure for the Federal Republic of Germany was 29.4 percent; that for France was 29.3 percent; and that for the United Kingdom only 22.4 percent.[4]

In general terms, most journalism training in Europe, with a few notable exceptions that will be discussed later, takes place outside a university environment. In the United States, almost all journalism education is conducted in universities, most of which offer a combination of practical training and theoretical courses in mass communication.

All the countries considered in this study do agree, however, that, in order to be effective, journalists must have two different kinds of competence. They must, first, be able to understand and interpret the social events with which they are confronted, and, second, they must have the specific skills necessary to convey this information to their audiences.[5] But, whereas in Europe it is assumed that students entering journalism training programs already possess a good general education, with many holding a university degree, in the United States journalism students are expected to take a mix of courses that include about 25 to 35 percent media studies and 65 to 75 percent arts and social sciences.

OVERVIEW

Before making a detailed analysis of journalism training in the United States, France and Great Britain, it might be useful to give a brief overview of the situation in each country both now and historically. In all three countries, journalism education is now facing the prospect of serious upheavals as the industry strives to understand and to react to the profound technological changes taking place in the field of mass communication. For the moment, education has one foot in the traditions of scissors and paste, and notebook and typewriter, and the other foot in the magical world of electronic editing and pagination, with even more mysterious and revolutionary techniques still to come.

With the profession changing so rapidly, teachers are likely to become out of date almost as soon as they start teaching. Consequently, it is increasingly difficult to shape programs to meet future needs because no one can tell what the profession will be like in ten years' time.

Historically, the United States has the oldest and strongest system of journalism education, dating back to the end of the nineteenth century.[6] After modest beginnings in such schools as Pennsylvania, Illinois and Missouri, journalism education in the United States soon gained strong support from the newspaper industry. Joseph Pulitzer of the *New York Daily World* gave $2 million to Columbia University to found the Pulitzer School of Journalism, which opened in 1912. In 1918, William J. Murphy, publisher of the *Minneapolis Tribune*, created an endowment fund for journalism education at the University of Minnesota. In 1921, the owners of the *Chicago Tribune* established the Medill School of Journalism at Northwestern University. Other schools and departments of journalism were created or developed with the help of state press associations and individuals.[7]

In France and Britain, journalism education developed more slowly. As is detailed below, the first French school of journalism was started in 1899 by a single individual. In Britain, formal journalism education did not begin until 1952 and was a joint initiative of the government, through the National Council for the Training of Journalists and the National Union of Journalists.

In the United States, journalism education has long succeeded in combining both journalism training and mass communication research into a valid field for university study. There has been something of a movement away from trade skills toward liberal arts studies, partly in response to demands from the industry. And now, there is a growing trend toward graduate education in journalism, which has created a need for more teachers with Ph.D. degrees. In the late 1950s, Wilbur Schramm was able to write: "Communication research has made a bridge between the professional strength or trade activities of schools and the ancient and intellectual strengths of the university."[8] Today, the bridge is starting to look a little shaky. The development of mass communication research at high theoretical levels may not have a direct effect upon undergraduate courses in journalism, but it must have some effect on journalism educators and the way in which they teach these courses. It would seem that the long-standing conflict between green eyeshade and chi-square is further than ever from being resolved.

In France, where serious journalism education dates back to the 1920s, the study of the mass media, particularly in the universities, has been influenced by a number of peculiarly French academic pursuits: structuralism, semiology and film. Although the Institut Français de Presse has successfully undertaken empirical studies of the French and foreign press from a political science perspective, most other university research in the field has been preoccupied with the psychological and physiological impact of messages or the symbolic structure of the mass media as creators of contemporary culture. French journalism skills training, as most editors and, indeed, journalists are happy to report, has kept well away from such preoccupations. On the other hand, despite increasing professionalism, French journalism is still very much attached to its literary traditions, and this is evident in the programs offered by journalism training institutions.

In Great Britain, formal journalism training and mass communication research have only emerged since World War II, despite some earlier attempts during the interwar period to introduce university level journalism education. Between 1919 and 1939, London University offered a two-year Journalism Diploma course, which produced a total of about 400 graduates, several of whom rose to important editorial positions at the *Times*, the *Observer* and the BBC.[9] Today, almost all training is given outside the universities, either in colleges of technology or, increasingly, in units run by individual newspapers. Training focuses mainly on professional skills with very little emphasis on theory, except for law. In the past, the NUJ (National Union of Journalists) has succeeded in keeping a very tight control over the training and "qualification" of journalists, to the point of achieving a virtual closed shop.

At the same time, the status of journalists has improved, particularly since the influx of increasing numbers of university graduates into the profession. Once journalists thought of themselves as little more than specialized journeymen. Today, they are more likely to seek a share of management and editorial policy. The phenomenon of "newsroom democracy" has become a reality in more than one Fleet Street publication.[10] In recent years, however, tensions have arisen between the NUJ and newspaper owners who wish to reserve the right to hire "unqualified" journalists, that is to say highly educated and specialized writers who have not gone through the hands of the NCTJ (National Council for the Training of Journalists). This conflict is still unresolved, but, resolved or not, it will continue to have a considerable impact on the way in which journalists are trained in Britain.[11]

WHERE JOURNALISM IS TAUGHT

In the United States, journalism is taught at more than 300 university schools and departments throughout the country, under the heading of journalism, communication, mass communications or media studies, to name just a few of the more common labels.[12] In any given year, 80,000 to 90,000 students are enrolled as journalism or mass communication majors. According to the 1983 Report of the Journalism Education Committee of the Associated Press Managing Editors (APME), an APME survey shows that editors say they are getting their best entry-level recruits from eighty-nine schools in different parts of the country. Although this survey has been criticized,[13] it does indicate the large number of schools providing satisfactory news staffers to the industry. The top five schools were found to be Missouri, Northwestern, Columbia, Kansas and Indiana, although not in any particular order.

About ninety schools are accredited by the Accrediting Council on Education in Journalism and Mass Communication (ACEJMC),[14] but as Bernard Redmont, then dean of the School of Public Communication at Boston College, pointed out in the 1984 Report of the APME Journalism Education Committee, some of the best and most respected schools, including Northwestern, Stanford, Michigan, the Annenberg School at Pennsylvania and Baylor, have voluntarily chosen not to participate in ACEJMC. Many other schools strongly promote ACEJMC's objectives, however.

In France, as indeed in most other countries around the world, the choice of schools offering journalism programs is much smaller than in the United States. *La Correspondance de la Presse* refers to fourteen schools in France, only half of which are accredited, or, more precisely, whose programs are "recognized by the Collective Convention on Journalists."[15] A government publication on professional training lists forty-nine institutions described as "schools of communication," but many of these are small private schools offering programs leading to diplomas well below the university degree level.[16]

The first journalism school in France, L'Ecole Supérieure de Journalisme, was founded in 1899 by an American woman living in Paris, Mrs. Dick May, about whom very little is known except that she imported the idea of journalism training from the United States, where the first schools had appeared a few years earlier. In 1900, the school was attached to the Ecole des Hautes Etudes en Sciences Sociales. According to communications scholar Bernard Voyenne, the school concentrated more on intellectual studies than training, and by all accounts was better fitted to produce publicists than journalists.[17] At the same time, another current of thought, of religious inspiration, sought to emphasize the moral foundations of journalism, and this led to the creation of the Ecole Supérieure de Journalisme de Lille, in 1924, as part of that city's Catholic University.

Today, the Lille school is still one of the best in France but never has more than about one hundred students. The most prestigious school is the Centre de Formation des Journalistes in Paris, set up in 1946 by representatives of the unions, the industry and the university. This school, which trains only fifty selected students at a time, has produced some of the best-known names in French journalism. The other two highly rated schools are L'Institut Universitaire de Technologie de Bordeaux, founded by the veteran journalist, teacher and writer, Robert Escarpit, and the Centre Universitaire d'Enseignement du Journalisme Strasbourg III. Although these four schools still consider themselves to be the best, a growing number of provincial universities are now starting to offer communications programs, in particular Tours, Rennes, Besançon and Lyons.

In Britain, the situation is different again. Training for newspaper journalism is carried out almost exclusively in the regional and local press under a scheme regulated and administered by the NCTJ, which was set up in 1952 mainly as a result of the 1949 Report of the Royal Commission on the Press. The NCTJ is concerned exclusively with newspaper journalists. Broadcast journalists have tended either to move into the electronic media from the newspapers or take the excellent training courses offered by the BBC. Since 1977, however, the London College of Printing has also offered broadcast training courses.[18]

NCTJ trainees, who are often already employed by a newspaper, attend courses accredited by the NCTJ. They can either attend part-time courses or take a one-year, full-time course at one of six colleges in England and Wales. These six colleges are Darlington College of Technology in Durham; Harlow College in Essex; Highbury College of Technology in Portsmouth; Lancashire Polytechnic in Preston; Richmond College in Sheffield; and South Glamorgan Institute of Higher Education in Cardiff, Wales. Postgraduate courses are offered at University College, Cardiff, City University in London and South Glamorgan Institute of Higher Learning in Cardiff. Accredited in-company training schemes are also run by six newspaper groups: Croydon Advertiser Group, Thomson Regional Newspapers, Express and Star in Wolverhampton, Westminster Press Ltd., Kent and Sussex Courier and Eastern Counties Newspapers Limited.[19]

It can be seen that journalism training is still a long way from being recognized as a university discipline even though a number of universities and polytechnics do offer degree courses in mass communications and media studies. The main reason for this is that journalism training in Europe focuses almost exclusively on skills. It is assumed that trainees already have a good level of general education. The proportion of new entrants to the NCTJ training scheme holding university degrees is steadily rising and is now more than 35 percent.

WHAT IS TAUGHT

In the United States, journalism educators, newspaper editors, media scholars and journalists periodically beat their breasts about the focus, value and efficacy of journalism training. While editors criticize journalism educators for failing to turn out graduates who can write, journalism educators complain that editors have too narrow a view of what constitutes journalism education. Although there is general agreement that a three-to-one balance of liberal arts and professional journalism courses is needed to produce well-educated, professionally prepared journalists, many editors refuse to recognize mass communication theory or media studies courses as part of the liberal arts curriculum.

In criticizing the "mass production and questionable education of journalists," media scholar Ben Bagdikian deplores the use of both "retired hacks" who have failed as journalists and Ph.D.s with little or no professional experience. He points out, though, that whatever editors and publishers say about journalism education, they continue to hire journalism graduates in ever-increasing numbers.[20]

There are other differences too, sometimes expressed with vehemence, but educators and professionals all seem to agree that the curricula should be modified. The Oregon Report describes the fundamental competencies that all journalism/mass communication graduates should have.[21] A model curriculum should include: (1) courses aimed at training in skills/craft competencies necessary for communicators generally; (2) conceptual knowledge courses that present the field of mass communication and its most vital component parts; and (3) professional modules aimed at acquaintance with the nuances and requirements of specific professional fields and industries.

Another future-oriented report, produced by the University of Missouri, argues that a solid grounding in the liberal arts, the ability to write, and some familiarity with the machinery are essentials, but it also goes on to state: "Increasingly, beginning journalists will need good backgrounds in the sciences and in computers." One respondent to the Missouri survey, Anthony Lewis of the *New York Times*, makes a plea for greater breadth of perspective: "We clearly are going to need more journalists trained in law and economics and business and so on. But we are also, urgently, going to need people who can keep and articulate a sense of the whole: a sense of values."[22]

There is considerable agreement as to what is needed. The

question is: When and how will it be achieved? Everette Dennis, who has written extensively about curriculum change refers to "a journalism education system that generally reflects little ability to adjust to change."[23] Dennis describes a curriculum written in 1928[24] and suggests that it could have been lifted verbatim from journalism school catalogs in the 1980s! Change may indeed be slow in coming.

In France, curricula are very closely matched to industry needs. The Centre de Formation des Journalistes in Paris, which offers a two-year program, has a curriculum that is typical of accredited schools. The first year is devoted to basic editorial and layout skills. Working alongside professional journalists, students do copy desk assignments, interviews and reporting. During the second term, these skills are applied to school newspapers. There is also a seven-week course on broadcast and news agency journalism. Over the summer vacation, students are required to do a two-month internship with a local newspaper. In keeping with the national convention on journalists, second-year students are considered as first-year professional probationers.

During this second year, they specialize in broadcast news, editing or agency work. At the same time, they take part in seminars on economics, politics, international relations and sports. To graduate, a good knowledge of English is also required.

A similar curriculum is offered at the Ecole Supérieure de Journalisme de Lille, although here rather more emphasis is placed on general knowledge, particularly during the first year when students have to take courses in political, economic and cultural aspects of the contemporary world; current affairs; the contemporary press in France and abroad; the history of information; and information law—as well as foreign languages and basic journalism skills such as news gathering and writing. During their second year, following a two-month internship with a provincial newspaper, students concentrate more on practical aspects of journalism but continue to develop their knowledge of current affairs, press law and economics.

Entry into these two schools is by competitive examination only, and, once in, the standards are high, but students are virtually guaranteed a job on graduation. The training given is decidedly professional but there is another aspect that is summed up by Daniel Junqua, the director-general of the Centre de Formation des Journalistes: "Beyond all the professional know-how and 'tricks of the trade,' our training never loses sight of the fact that a journalist is first and foremost a free man who looks on people and facts with a critical eye, who refuses all kinds of ready-made thoughts, but who should never cultivate detachment or cynicism."[25]

In Britain too, training is very much industry driven. In order to become fully qualified, journalists must complete six preliminary NCTJ examinations, a shorthand test, and a final proficiency test. Each year, the proficiency test is taken by about 650 reporters and 35 photographers. On an average, 70 percent of the reporters and 85 percent of the photographers pass the test. According to the NCTJ, the aims of the newspaper journalism syllabus are to enable trainees:

- To recognize, obtain and select important, relevant and newsworthy facts from either written or verbal sources, using appropriate skills or techniques
- To write clear, vigorous and balanced reports in a form that will attract and interest the reader
- To gain a general knowledge of a newspaper's departments (for instance production, advertising, circulation and finance, as well as editorial) and an understanding of the industry's structure and economics.[26]

In order to acquire these skills, trainees take courses in news gathering and processing, writing, reporting, law, public administration and the role of the newspaper in society. In all these courses, the main emphasis is on practical skills. For example, in the law courses trainees are taught not only about libel and defamation but also how to understand and interpret legal proceedings. Similarly, in reporting courses, they are taught how to ask questions, make use of shorthand and to address members of the clergy, aristocracy and civic leaders. Law courses are particularly detailed because British journalists are not protected by anything like the U.S. First Amendment and are, as a consequence, far more vulnerable to legal action. Finally, it should be stressed that, under the British system, considerably more attention is given to on-the-job training than in either France or the United States. This may explain why, in Britain, journalism is considered more as a craft than a profession.

WHO TEACHES JOURNALISM

In the United States, the question of who teaches journalism is one that is fraught with controversy, mainly because it is taught in universities. Universities require certain academic credentials of journalism educators, while industry insists on professional experience. It has been said that the ideal journalism professor should have a Ph.D., with a strong record of scholarly publications, twenty years as a professional with a prestigious news organization and a Pulitzer Prize. In Europe, there is less of a problem because journalism is usually taught in specialized schools. European universities, if they deal with journalism at all, concentrate on the more theoretical aspects of the communication process.

In France, partly because of a strong tradition of literary journalism, journalists and teachers seem to be able to move very freely between journalism and the university. One striking example is Robert Escarpit who not only founded the Bordeaux journalism program but who also wrote a front-page column for *Le Monde* for thirty years, as well as producing more than fifty books and leading an active political life. As a consequence of this situation, French journalism schools have no difficulty in attracting working journalists to teach practices. Furthermore, as they are unhampered by the exigencies of academic research they can concentrate wholly on the task at hand.

The situation is somewhat similar in Britain in that much of the training is given on the job by working professionals. While this kind of apprenticeship training virtually guarantees the preservation of journalistic traditions, it does little to stimulate critical appraisal of the profession. College teaching is provided by full-time lecturers who are nearly always former journalists. The obvious exceptions are teachers giving courses in law and public administration. Here again, since formal training is given in colleges of technology rather than universities, educators do not necessarily have to hold advanced degrees.

WHO STUDIES JOURNALISM

Weaver and Wilhoit's portrait of U.S. news people, *The American Journalist*, shows that, in 1983, 40 percent of all U.S. journalists had majored in journalism and that almost three-fourths of them were college graduates.[27] In 1987, journalism schools produced 21,100 graduates. Of these, 47.1 percent found media-related jobs. However, 39.1 percent of these new hires were in public relations and advertising. In other words, only 28.7 percent of the year's journalism/communication graduates entered what could be defined as journalistic jobs in newspapers, broadcasting or periodicals.[28]

This situation is quite different from Europe, where a high percentage of French journalism students, and the quasi-totality of all British journalism students find employment as journalists. However, Weaver and Wilhoit conclude that, in the United States, formal training in journalism is becoming a necessary condition for entry into the news media.[29]

Perhaps because of confidentiality rulings affecting student survey questionnaires, and also because of a lack of research in this area, there appears to be a total dearth of information regarding the socioeconomic background of U.S. journalism majors. Virtually all that can be deduced from available data is that 99 percent are white, 60 percent female and most come from fairly affluent middle-class families. Among minority groups, which continue to grow, although at a very slow rate, females outnumber males almost two to one.

In Britain, which has about 27,000 full-time journalists, the industry recruits some 600 trainees each year, a figure that is down from a peak of 840 in 1975.[30] Most start on weekly newspapers as direct entrants. About a quarter take a one-year, full-time course in newspaper journalism at one of six colleges. Twenty years ago, most of these recruits came from middle-and lower-middle-class families.[31] Only 12 percent were university graduates. As has already been mentioned, the number of graduates entering journalism today has risen to an estimated 35 percent. Since there is a close correlation between social origin and university education in Britain, it could be conjectured that the social level of journalists is also rising. However, it should be pointed out that many university graduates are recruited directly into London-based newspapers. Trainees joining provincial newspapers are still likely to be of modest social origin.

According to the French Press Card Commission, there are some 21,000 journalists working in France. The commission issues about 1,000 new cards every year, but since this figure includes probationers and part-time employees, as well as such categories as cameraman, "reporter-illustrator" and "stenographer-writer," the number of full-time professionals entering the industry is probably much lower. The proportion of cardholders employed as full-fledged permanent journalists is approximately 65 percent, so it might be reasonable to assume that the actual number of full-time journalists entering the profession each year is in the region of 650.

With regard to social origin, the Press Card Commission has gathered information about the occupation of journalists' fathers, shown in Table 1.[32]

Table 1
Occupation of Fathers of French Journalists

Father's occupation	Journalists		
	Men	Women (percentages) (n = 8400)	Average
Farmer	3.0	2.0	2.8
Craftsman/shopkeeper	10.0	10.9	10.2
Professional/executive	17.7	27.1	20.0
Middle management	10.1	9.4	9.9
Office worker	6.6	4.1	6.0
Hourly worker	6.7	5.1	6.3
Domestic employee	0.7	1.0	0.7
Journalist	8.3	4.4	7.3
Industrialist	1.3	2.4	1.6
Others actively employed	3.4	4.5	3.7
Not actively employed	11.9	9.9	11.4
No response	20.3	19.2	20.1
	100.0	100.0	100.0

FUTURE TRENDS IN JOURNALISM EDUCATION

In all three countries, journalism education has been the subject of criticism from publishers and editors, academics and also journalists. Reasons for criticism may vary from country to country but they have all produced the same result: a desire to modify and improve existing structures.

In the United States, the Oregon Report, already referred to, concluded that "the general state of journalism and mass communication education is dismal." The principal causes of this dismal state were identified as lack of funding, continuing large enrollments and small, overworked faculties. The curriculum reforms discussed above may lead to better results, but, for the moment, the main complaint seems to be that existing curricula are not producing well-rounded individuals. "We have a lot of journalists who know *how* to write," Guido Stempel states in the report, "but they don't know *what* to write." Stempel believes that too many issues and events in society are covered so superficially that the coverage is meaningless.

In the same report, David Eason suggests that the major function of journalism education should be to produce a thinking journalist who is skilled rather than a mere skilled journalist. "The end goal of our programs should be to make our students more curious about the world rather than self-satisfied that a few writing techniques are all one needs to cope with the complexities of contemporary society." Wise words, but they may be an indictment more of general educational levels in American universities than of specific journalism programs.

In France, a good level of general education is sometimes more highly prized than formal training in a journalism school. The results of a survey published in *Le Monde de l'Education* show that of 684 journalists hired between 1980 and 1984, 74 percent had received university training, but only 40 percent were graduates of accredited journalism schools.[33] Of those having received university training, 25 percent had completed literary or social science studies, 17 percent political science, 21 percent law, 13 percent languages, 11 percent history, 9 percent economics, and 4 percent science. By way of comparison, Weaver and Wilhoit's survey of U.S. journalists in 1982–83 shows that of those who had received a college education, 54.7 percent had majored in communication subjects, including 39.8 percent in journalism, and 40.2 percent in liberal arts and sciences, including 14.7 percent in English, 6.3 percent in history and 4.9 percent in political science, with only 0.1 percent having studied law.[34]

The recent explosion of new audio-visual techniques and local "free" radio stations in France has created a heavy demand for trained personnel, and this has led to the introduction of new "communication programs" in all sorts of educational establishments. This has been criticized by the French union of journalists which continues to approve only a limited number of schools. *Le Journaliste* cautions against the kind of excess that produced too many "human science" graduates in the 1960s and too many computer technicians in the 1970s.[35]

Whatever the attacks made against journalism education in France, the trend is definitely toward expansion. Newspapers no longer have the time to do traditional on-the-job training. While entry-level graduates of journalism schools are far from being experienced professionals, they are immediately operational and, in the eyes of editors, that is their strength.[36] This trend is further confirmed by the fact that in 1984 approximately 10 percent of all working journalists were journalism graduates, while less than a year later statistics from the French Press Card Commission revealed that 23 percent of all new recruits had undergone journalism training, which shows that schools of journalism are playing an increasingly important role in the profession.[37]

In Britain, the main concern in journalism education is with the kind of recruit entering the system. Although more and more university graduates are coming into the profession, general standards seem to be lower than they once were. Former editor Colin Brannigan believes that staff shortages are making it too easy to achieve senior status and that "many youngsters entering journalism today do so with a view to moving into radio, television or public relations, where the money is more attractive."[38] Fleet Street no longer holds the attraction it once did. Television is now the first choice of both established and entry-level journalists, and provincial newspapers are finding it very difficult to hold on to trained staff.

The 1977 Royal Commission on the Press (the McGregor Report) found that while much progress had been made since the 1947–49 commission, a great deal still remained to be done. In particular, it recommended that basic training should include more knowledge of local and central government, as well as political, industrial and social affairs. It concluded that "qualified journalists should have more access to advanced professional education."[39]

John Dodge, a former director of the NCTJ, sees part of the answer in an "overdue partnership" between industry and the universities.[40] Looking into the future, Dodge believes that London's City University could become journalism's "center of excellence" in the academic world provided it can develop: (1) a strong and prestigious postgraduate course; (2) a center for older and more experienced journalists, from all parts of the media; and (3) an international center coordinating the current efforts of organizations such as the International Press Institute and the Thomson Foundation. But, until further funding can be found, such a project must remain in the realm of speculation.

CONCLUSION

The way in which journalism training has developed in the United States, France and Great Britain has been largely influenced by the attitudes that the public, educators and journalists themselves have had about the profession. At the same time, the objectives and priorities of journalism education have continued to perpetuate popular images of the profession. While journalistic practices are beginning to change in each country as they move toward a more uniform pattern, there are still marked divergences in the images fostered by journalism training.

In the United States, only 17 percent of the journalists interviewed by Weaver and Wilhoit felt that their role should be an adversarial one.[41] And yet there is still the myth of the journalist as watchdog, as champion and defender of freedoms and the First Amendment, whose primary purpose of gathering and distributing news and opinion is to serve the general welfare by informing the people and enabling them to make judgments on the issues of the time.[42] Contrary to what professionals themselves believe,[43] in *popular imagination*, the American journalist is still a searcher after truth so "that the people shall know."

In Britain, on the other hand, the journalist is still viewed as a not very gentlemanly gentleman of the press, as a skillful craftsman capable of uncovering and reporting the facts, but also not above embellishing them to make a better story. Stanley Cohen, who is editor of *Focus* magazine in London, has identified a distinctive British attitude toward the role of newspapers, which he sees as "quasi-commercial" entities. Although they have been forced to accept advertising as a source of revenue, they still yearn for the days when newspapers were instruments of political power in the hands of owners and editors.[44]

In France, the journalist is above all a writer and commentator, honest about facts perhaps, but less interested in their intrinsic worth than what can be made of them. Bernard Voyenne describes the journalist in these terms: "A translator and yet not an author, an ever-present witness on the stage and yet never truly an actor, an explainer of things rather than a teacher, this midwife of reality holds up to society the mirror without which it would be nothing more than a frozen monster, without a mouth, without ears, and without a soul."[45]

Partly because of these images and partly because of journalistic habits and traditions, each country has developed its own order of priorities, its own set of professional values and its own system of training. However, even if, in practice, there are differences in the way in which news is *interpreted* or used, journalism curricula and training methods demonstrate a large measure of agreement over what actually constitutes news.

NOTES

1. Georges Bohère, *Profession: Journalist* (Geneva: ILO, 1984); May Katzen, *Mass Communication: Teaching and Studies at Universities* (Paris: UNESCO Press, 1975); UNESCO, *Training for Mass Communication*, Reports and Papers on Mass Communication (Paris: UNESCO, 1975); Ramon Sala-Balust, "Journalists' Training: A FIEJ Survey," in *FIEJ Bulletin* 144, September 30, 1985, pp. 9–12.

2. Lee Becker, Jeffrey Fruit and Susan Caudill, with Sharon Dunwoody and Leonard Tipton, *The Training and Hiring of Journalists* (Norwood, N.J.: Ablex, 1987).

3. Bertrand and Urabayen, "European Mass Media in the 1980s," p. 28.

4. *The UNESCO Statistical Yearbook* (Paris: UNESCO, 1987).

5. Katzen, *Training for Mass Communication*, p. 9.

6. Frank Luther Mott, *American Journalism, A History: 1690–1960*, 3d ed. (New York: Macmillan, 1982), pp. 604–605.

7. Emery and Emery, *The Press and America*, pp. 581–582.

8. Wilbur Schramm, "The State of Communication Research," *Public Opinion Quarterly* 23:6 (Spring 1959), p. 17.

9. Frederic N. Hunter, "Grub Street and Academia: The Relationship between Journalism and Education, 1880–1940" (Ph.D. dissertation, City University, London, 1984).

10. The most striking case is that of the *New Statesman*, the London weekly, in which journalists obtained the agreement of the board to elect the editor of their choice.

11. This became an issue with the London *Observer* which, in a memorandum attached to a house agreement signed with the National Union of Journalists on February 13, 1970, agreed to "inform" rather than "consult" the NUJ in advance of the appointment of an "unqualified" journalist.

12. David Weaver and G. Cleveland Wilhoit, "A Profile of JMC Educators: Traits, Attitudes and Values," *Journalism Educator* 43:2 (Summer 1988), p. 6.

13. In particular James Carey in a report to APME on behalf of the Association of Schools of Journalism and Mass Communications.

14. Ninety-one accredited programs are listed in the 1988 *Journalism and Mass Communication Directory* (Columbia, SC.: Association for Education in Journalism and Mass Communication, 1988), p. 70.

15. *La correspondance de la presse* (two documentary studies dated August 1 and August 8, 1986, communicated to the author by the Institut Français de Presse).

16. Isabelle Hernett, "Les écoles de communication," *EPP*, June 16, 1986, pp. 60–64.

17. Bernard Voyenne, *Les journalistes français: d'où viennent-ils? Qui sont-ils? Que font-ils?* (Paris: Les Editions CFPJ, 1985), pp. 227–228.

18. Personal communication from Frederic N. Hunter, London College of Printing, February 23, 1989.

19. *Training for Newspaper Journalism* (London: The Newspaper Society, n.d.).

20. Benjamin H. Bagdikian, "Woodstein U: Notes on the Mass Production and Questionable Education of Journalists," *Atlantic* 239:3 (1977), pp. 81–92.

21. *Planning for Curricular Change*, a report of the Project on the Future of Journalism and Mass Communications Education (Eugene: School of Journalism, University of Oregon, 1984), p. 82.

22. *Communications 1990*, a report of the Future Committee (Columbia, Missouri: School of Journalism, University of Columbia-Missouri, 1980).

23. Everette Dennis, "Journalism Education: Failing Grades from a Dean," *ASNE Bulletin*, October 1983, p. 27.

24. *What is Taught in Schools of Journalism* (University of Missouri Journalism Series Bulletin 54, 1928).

25. Daniel Junqua, foreword to the 1987 Brochure of the Centre de Formation des Journalistes (Paris: CFPJ, 1987).

26. *Newspaper Journalism Syllabus: Aims* (London: National Council for the Training of Journalists, May 1984).

27. David H. Weaver and G. Cleveland Wilhoit, *The American Journalist: A Portrait of U.S. News People and Their Work* (Bloomington: Indiana University Press, 1986). See the whole of Chapter 3, "Education and Training," pp. 41–64.

28. The Dow Jones Newspaper Fund, *1988 Journalism Career and Scholarship Guide* (Princeton, N.J.: Dow Jones Newspaper Fund, 1988), pp. 12–13.

29. Weaver and Wilhoit, *The American Journalist*, p. 54.

30. Colin Brannigan, "Training: The Greatest Problem Facing the Industry," in *The British Press* (London: The Commonwealth Press Union, 1981), pp. 66–68.

31. Tunstall, *Journalists at Work*, pp. 60–61.

32. This information is based on a survey conducted jointly by the French Press Card Commission and the French Center for Public Opinion Research in 1982. Questionnaires were sent out with card renewal notices to about 18,000 cardholders; 8,400 responses were received.

33. "Les patrons préfèrent embaucher des universitaires," *Le Journaliste* 194 (February-March 1985), p. 3.

34. Weaver and Wilhoit, *The American Journalist*, p. 56.

35. "Formation ou charlatanisme?" *Le Journaliste* 193 (August-September 1984), p. 6.

36. Bénédicte Haquin, "Les entreprises de presse: des employeurs insatisfaits," *Presse-Actualité* (June-July 1985), p. 24.

37. Jean Savary, "Les écoles de journalisme: permis de conduire ou leçon de conduite?" *Presse-Actualité* (June-July 1985), p. 19.

38. Brannigan, "Training," pp. 67–68.

39. *Royal Commission on the Press: Final Report* (London: HMSO, 1977), p. 180.

40. John Dodge, "An Overdue Partnership," in *The British Press* (London: The Commonwealth Press Union, 1981), pp. 70–71.

41. Weaver and Wilhoit, *The American Journalist*, p. 123.

42. "A Statement of Principles," American Society of Newspaper Editors, October 23, 1975.

43. Weaver and Wilhoit, *The American Journalist*, p. 116.

44. Stanley Cohen, letter to the editor of *Quill*, October 1986, p. 4.

45. Bernard Voyenne, *Les journalistes français*, p. 266.

4

RECENT DEVELOPMENTS

Since World War II, journalism in France, Britain and the United States has been strongly influenced by two seemingly irresistible trends: increasing competition and the concentration of media ownership. These phenomena have led to a number of other changes in media funding, editorial policies, staffing and journalistic procedures. They in turn have produced or been accompanied by major technological developments in news gathering and processing, production methods and distribution, as well as new readership patterns. At the same time, new media have appeared, adding more fuel to an already overheated climate of competition.

These various changes have taken place in each country at different times, at different speeds and in different circumstances. This makes it difficult to track them with precision but, on the whole, despite the fact that each of the three countries is currently at a different stage of development, the results appear to be very similar. There is evidence to suggest that the changes brought about by increased competition and concentration of ownership are having a homogenizing effect upon journalistic practices and media content. This chapter attempts to explain some of the changes that have already taken place, and to identify others that are waiting in the wings.

The fact that many of these changes have occurred at different times in France, Britain and the United States may be explained by some major differences that have emerged in these countries since World War II. These differences are historical, economic, structural and cultural.

Historically, the press systems of all three countries were seriously affected by the war, but in different ways. France was invaded and split into two zones. Newspapers either resisted or collaborated with the German occupying forces in the north, or the Vichy government in the south. At the Liberation, in a dramatic settling of accounts, most newspapers were wrested from private ownership, renamed and entrusted to the hands of those editors who had shown the most resistance or who had been active in the clandestine press. Not only were many titles lost during the war but the public's confidence in the press faded, encouraging the rapid development of radio.[1]

Britain, although never occupied, had to face the threat of invasion and the reality of bombardment. At times, as the country stood alone against the German war machine, the press, and radio too, played a vital role in maintaining the morale and determination of the British people, and, no doubt for this reason, enjoyed considerable popularity. The national press in particular prospered. Despite newsprint shortages and fewer pages, the circulation of the London papers rose from eighteen million to twenty-three million during the war years.[2]

The United States entered the war later than its European allies and, although it was fully committed to a total war effort, the hostilities never really threatened its national territory. Nor did it suffer from the chronic newsprint shortages that hampered the European press. But the U.S. press did lose about 130 titles during the war and it did lose ground to radio, which, with Ed Murrow's famous broadcasts from war-torn London and elsewhere, proved that it was capable of coverage of live events thousands of miles away. Perhaps the most traumatic circumstance for the U.S. media, however, was that, like their European counterparts, they were subjected to censorship and a degree of government control, which, even if similar controls had already been applied during World War I, ran contrary to the most fundamental principles of American journalism.[3] This would have an effect on how Americans thought about news and news-people.

POSTWAR RECOVERY

When the war ended, the media were also affected by the speed with which the economies of their respective countries were able to rebuild themselves. The U.S. economy, which had suffered relatively little during the war, rebounded vigorously despite some sporadic labor unrest. The U.S. press followed suit, supported by rapidly increasing advertising revenues which off-set soaring newsprint costs, rising postal rates and higher wages. In Europe, sluggish economic recovery in the immediate postwar years did little to stimulate the demand for advertising, and, even when prosperity started to return in the 1950s, rising pro-duction costs forced newspapers to increase prices thereby flat-tening the growth of readership.

The buoyancy of the American economy encouraged publish-ers to invest in new technology that enabled them to produce newspapers more cheaply and with fewer workers. In Britain and France, such investment did not become possible until much later, partly because of slower economic growth and partly be-cause of an unfavorable political climate. Indeed, both countries had returned left-wing governments to power as soon as the war ended. In Britain, the lack of capital investment was also the result of a certain smugness over British performance during the war.

Furthermore, media usage remained very different. Whereas in the United States radio networks had already established themselves as national news vehicles in the late 1930s, in France and Britain national newspapers continued to maintain high readerships. Indeed, until the late 1960s and early 1970s, when price increases forced choices to be made, it was not uncommon for British families to take two morning nationals, as well as morning and evening locals. The situation in France was not quite this extreme, but Paris morning papers had good pene-tration in the provinces. All in all, since those postwar years, some of the differences between France, Britain and the United States have become more accentuated. Others have disappeared.

On the whole, since the war, the number of daily newspapers in the United States has declined slightly, but overall circulations have risen by about 23 percent, partly because of population increases. In 1946, there were a total of 1,763 daily newspapers. By 1987 this figure had dropped to 1,645, a decline of just over 6 percent. During the same time period, however, the number of morning newspapers increased dramatically from 334 to 512, a jump of 53 percent, while the number of evening newspapers fell from 1,429 to 1,165, a decline of almost 20 percent. Meanwhile, combined circulations rose from about 51 million to 63 million.[4]

The number of pages has also risen during the same period mainly because of advertising.[5] This growth has taken place despite competition from other media, television in particular. Most newspapers in the United States, however, must be thought of as local publications with strong advertising support from the communities they serve. Even such giants as the *Los Angeles Times* and the *Chicago Tribune* are essentially city papers and rely heavily on local advertising. The vast majority of U.S. newspapers have circulations of under 50,000 and are very profitable.

One notable exception—on several counts—is Gannett's *USA Today*, which set out to become a national newspaper but which, by the end of 1986, was said to have lost $380 million in four and a half years.[6] However, the newspaper saw its first profitable month in May 1987, six months ahead of projections, and at the end of the first quarter of 1988 the Audit Bureau of Circulations showed an average daily paid circulation of 1,631,335 making *USA Today* the second largest daily newspaper in the United States.[7]

In both France and Britain newspaper circulations have declined steadily since the end of the war. In Britain, overall circulations have dropped by about 5 percent in the last twenty years, with the largest losses being sustained by the London morning papers.[8] The situation is very similar in France where overall circulations have dropped by over 10 percent while the Paris newspapers have lost almost half their postwar circulation.[9] On the whole, the "quality" newspapers in both countries have fared better than the popular press. London has even seen the birth of a new upmarket London morning, the *Independent*, while in Paris *Le Monde* continues to be a success, as does the trendy *Libération*. The London dailies are still very much national newspapers read throughout the country, but in France the big Paris papers have lost much of their provincial readership. It is significant that the largest newspaper in France today is *Ouest-France*, published in Rennes, Brittany, with a circulation of around 850,000.

Meanwhile, the provincial press in both Britain and France has suffered from rising production costs and concentration of ownership. At the end of the war, France had 175 regional newspapers which, at first, were very successful, adding more than nine million in circulation between 1945 and 1946 alone. However, by the end of the decade many of them were losing ground rapidly. Between 1946 and 1954, some sixty provincial dailies disappeared. The law of August 2, 1954, restored a number of newspaper properties to their former owners who had been stripped of their rights by the law of May 11, 1946. The new law also allowed once again the acquisition of newspaper properties that had been transferred to the state under the 1946 law. These new dispositions paved the way for the phenomenon of group ownership, which has seen the emergence of three major groups: the Hersant group, the Amaury group and the Hachette-Filipacchi group. In the wake of this phenomenon, many other titles disappeared. Between 1960 and 1977 almost thirty provincial dailies died, and today only about seventy-five remain.[10]

In Britain, the provincial press found itself in a weakened state immediately following the war, but continued to survive thanks to the loyalty of its readers. When the economy gradually recovered, British readers continued to buy one or two local newspapers every day, but as production costs rose and competition for advertising revenue increased, it soon became obvious that, before long, there would be too many newspapers for too few readers. The first casualties were the provincial evening papers.

NEW GROUP OWNERSHIP

In 1959, Roy Thomson acquired Kemsley Newspapers, which marked the beginning of a period of concentration of ownership, and, as titles continued to disappear, less competition. Ten years later, 55 percent of all provincial newspapers in Britain were owned by press groups, including the Thomson Organization, but also the News of the World Organization, Associated Newspapers, United Newspapers and Westminster Press.

By the mid 1960s, the provincial press was dominated by large evening newspapers in the major industrial cities. There were a few successful morning newspapers and a larger number of less successful morning newspapers supported by affluent evening papers. There were also hundreds of very prosperous weeklies. Today, there are fewer evening papers and their overall circulation has dropped by 28 percent. Five of the big city evening papers have declined by 43 percent. Since 1980, when the London *Evening News* finally disappeared, there has not been a single town in Britain supporting two evening papers.[11]

There are, however, growing signs that British newspapers may be entering a new phase of expansion. The *Independent*, launched in 1986, has developed to the point where it now offers a formidable challenge to such well-established titles as the *Times*, the *Guardian*, and the *Daily Telegraph*. In August 1988, the publishers of the venerable Scottish daily, the *Scotsman*, launched a full-fledged Sunday newspaper designed to compete with such heavyweights as Rupert Murdoch's *Sunday Times*, the *Observer*, and the *Sunday Telegraph*, which are already engaged in a battle for "quality" readers. The *Guardian* has started a new edition in Frankfurt, West Germany, while Robert Maxwell is currently planning a new daily, the *European*, to be distributed widely in continental Europe.

Perhaps the most significant event of 1988, however, was the launching of the *North West Times* in Manchester, in late September. This is the first new regional morning newspaper to appear this century. What is particularly significant about this event is that, because of new production technology and the greatly reduced influence of the print unions, the *North West Times* will apparently require only 50,000 subscribers to break even. The newspaper was started with a capital investment of $3.6 million and a staff of only fifty journalists. It seems that changed economic conditions now make it possible for new titles to compete vigorously with established rivals.[12]

Patterns of group ownership have developed somewhat differently in France, Britain, and the United States. To be sure, before and after World War I, all three countries had their press "barons"—in France Prouvost and Coty, in Britain Northcliffe and Beaverbrook, in the United States Hearst and Scripps, all of whom founded powerful press businesses. Since then, in France and Britain, press moguls Robert Hersant, Rupert Murdoch and Robert Maxwell have built their own private media empires. While these empires are run on a day-to-day basis by corporate functionaries, the style, personality and individual convictions of these three controversial figures can be seen in editorial and administrative policies. However, in the United States, media ownership has passed largely, but not exclusively, from private hands to corporate control. About 75 percent of all dailies are now owned by chains, or groups as they prefer to be called. Corporate administrative policies are less idiosyncratic than those of the moguls. Although management styles may differ, the end results, dictated by profit maximization, are identical. Whether ownership is in the hands of Gannett or Scripps-Howard, Hersant or Hachette, Murdoch or Maxwell, the same "improvements" tend to be made: streamlining of management, imposition of profit objectives, pooling of technical and editorial resources, reduction of personnel and, generally, a move down-market.

Another feature that characterizes group ownership, whether it be corporate or individual, is that, in all three countries, it is spreading its financial net in ever-wider circles. Initially, press groups were content to buy up radio and television stations, weeklies, magazines and other competing media. Today, their financial interests have spread to cable systems, newsprint manufacturing, timberlands and trucking. In Europe, in particular, media groups now own interests in publishing, oil, banking, entertainment, manufacturing and other activities unrelated to the media. It could be argued that such diversification provides greater financial strength to the group, and, on more than one occasion, losing newspapers have been subsidized by profits from nonmedia holdings. On the other hand, because of this diversification, decisions governing the future of individual news organizations may be influenced by factors foreign, and

perhaps hostile, to the media. The dangers of "interlocking
directorates"[13] and a "private ministry of information"[14] have
been well documented.

INTERNATIONALIZATION

A parallel development in patterns of group ownership has
been internationalization. Rupert Murdoch's group, News International, owns substantial media holdings not only in his
native Australia, but also in Great Britain and the United States.
Murdoch's interest in the U.S. market is so great that he has
taken out U.S. citizenship in order to comply with federal rulings
governing the ownership of television stations. He also owns
the European cable system Skychannel and has book publishing
interests in the Netherlands.[15]

Robert Maxwell's communications group employs 15,000 people in sixteen countries. Apart from owning the Mirror Group
Newspapers, which represents a sizeable piece of the British
market, Maxwell is also Europe's biggest printer and has numerous publishing, printing and television joint ventures in
other parts of the world including Japan, Kenya and Bulgaria.
Maxwell, who was born in Czechoslovakia, and who is married
to a French woman, has large holdings in the French TF–1 channel and the Agence Centrale de Presse news agency. As has
already been mentioned, he hopes to start a Paris-based English
language daily called the *European* for distribution throughout
Europe. Maxwell's future plans involve media acquisitions in
the United States, where he already owns substantial printing
interests.[16]

In France, the internationalization of group ownership has
been slow. Of the French groups, Hachette is the most international with subsidiaries or affiliates in more than forty countries, including the United States.[17] Hersant, who in recent years
has been burdened with huge bank loans, heavy overheads and
substantial losses incurred by his involvement in La Cinq television channel, has just not been able to borrow the cash to
extend his holdings overseas. Nor, like most French media
groups, has he had the inclination.[18] However, if there has been
relatively little internationalization of group ownership in

France, at least from the inside out, there has been considerable foreign investment in the French media, particularly since 1982 when the law on broadcast communication eradicated the last remnants of government control and paved the way for the privatization of television.[19] As already stated, Maxwell has large holdings in French media organizations, and, recently, the financial daily *Les Echos* was acquired by the British group, Pearson, in which, incidentally, Murdoch now has more than a 20 percent interest.

American media groups are far less inclined to seek holdings in foreign media. However, at least one group—Gannett—has demonstrated international ambitions in attempting to market *USA Today* overseas. Also, as in France, foreign investors are acquiring segments of the U.S. communications industry. Murdoch now owns two newspapers, more than twenty magazines, seven television stations, the Twentieth Century Fox studio and Harper and Row, the book publisher.[20] Maxwell has acquired a string of printing plants and is now the second largest printer in the United States, printing mostly newspaper inserts and magazines. He has already attempted, unsuccessfully, to buy the *New York Post*, *Scientific American*, and the publishing company of Harcourt Brace Jovanovich, and there is little doubt that he will go on shopping until he is successful in acquiring properties in magazine, book or newspaper publishing.[21] Finally, when UPI experienced grave financial difficulties in the mid-1980s, at least one foreign group showed a strong interest in buying it out.

It can be seen from the above, then, that media ownership in France, Britain and the United States is becoming more concentrated, more diversified and more international. Today, with multimedia ownership, foreign capitalization and interlocking directorates, decisions concerning the future of media vehicles, or their editorial policies, may not always be taken with the interests of the media, or the public, at heart. Furthermore, new management styles, production methods and news processing technology, introduced with the purpose of maximizing profit, are resulting in uniform coverage and generic layouts. The other major trend, mentioned at the beginning of the chapter, alongside concentration of ownership, is competition.

COMPETITION

Competition has long been at the very heart of the newspaper business. Almost as soon as high-speed printing technology made it possible to print as many copies as could be sold, competition among newspapers deteriorated into outright warfare. Some of the bloodiest battlefields were the capital cities of France, Britain and the United States. In New York, which had twenty-two dailies in 1910, Hearst's *Journal* vied for readership with Pulitzer's *World*. In London, which before World War I had some eighteen daily newspapers, it was Northcliffe of the *Mail* who did battle with Beaverbrook of the *Express*, soon to be joined by Rothermere of the *Mirror*. But it was in Paris, which in 1910 had sixty dailies, that competition was the most intense. France at that period had the largest circulations in the world, and, in the French capital, four newspapers, *Le Petit Journal*, *Le Petit Parisien*, *Le Matin* and *Le Journal*, together sold more than four million copies every day.[22]

This kind of competition has continued, to a certain extent, in Paris and London, and to a lesser degree in New York. Outside these major metropolitan areas, however, competition among newspapers has generally been reduced or eliminated altogether by the disappearance of unsuccessful titles or the purchase of competing newspapers by the same owner. Meanwhile, further competition has come from the once "new" media of radio and television.

Radio news bulletins were immediately perceived as a threat to newspapers. The first newscast, which, in fact, consisted only of election returns, was broadcast in the United States in 1920 from Pittsburgh. In the absence of federal regulation, radio stations sprang up all across the country, despite vigorous protests from newspaper publishers. Ultimately, some of this tension was resolved when newspaper owners bought financial interests in the new radio stations.[23] In Britain, the first news bulletin was broadcast by the BBC in 1923, but the press succeeded in obtaining legislation that prohibited the broadcasting of news before seven in the evening. In France, the first news program was broadcast from Privat in 1925. Here too, as in the United States, press interests failed to do little more than retard the development of radio news and solved the issue by creating or buying into radio stations. This was never the case in Britain where the BBC had a monopoly. By 1939 there were 5.2 million radio sets in France, 9.8 million in Britain, and 31 million in the United States.[24]

For many listeners, radio was primarily a source of entertainment, but the war established it as a bona fide news medium. Radio and newspapers soon found they could coexist, even if radio had appropriated forever a healthy slice of available advertising revenues, at least in the United States. Above all, the two media learned to fulfill separate functions. While radio was able to provide spot news and live coverage, newspapers were better equipped to provide explanation and commentary. This was less true in France and Britain where commercial broadcasting was much slower to emerge and where national newspapers continued to act as primary news sources, thus maintaining their grip on advertising.

When, however, production costs started to skyrocket in the 1950s and 1960s and when television began to emerge as a major medium, first in the United States and then, gradually, in Britain and France, newspapers found themselves in a state of disarray. American newspapers, already largely supported by cross-ownership agreements and group financial strength, were in a better position to survive than their European counterparts, which may explain, at least in part, why they have lost fewer titles and actually gained circulation. When, in the late 1970s, French and British newspapers suffered the onslaught of renewed competition from commercial radio, and, above all, freesheets, they found themselves faced with dwindling readerships and a smaller share of available advertising revenue. While some French and British newspapers are still fighting for survival, there now seem to be indications of returning strength in the newspaper industry, particularly in Britain.[25]

The responses of newspaper owners to these various waves of competition have been the same in all three countries, but, because of time lags in social, economic and technological developments, the responses have occurred at different intervals. The first reaction has been chain ownership. Indeed, the simplest method of dealing with a competing newspaper or radio station is to buy it so as to absorb it into a widened financial base.

In the United States, this began much earlier than in Europe. By the late 1920s, there were already about sixty chains in the United States, involving some 300 newspapers and accounting for about one third of total daily newspaper circulation.[26] Serious group ownership did not really start in Britain until well after World War II, with Roy Thomson and Cecil King, and, in France, apart from the existence of some powerful press families, it has taken a Robert Hersant to develop the notion of newspaper chains. Although Hersant has been building his empire since the 1950s, it could be argued that he did not really hit his stride until 1975 when he acquired the venerable Paris daily, *Le Figaro*.[27] However, all in all, although the extent and speed of development of chain ownership have been somewhat different in France, Britain and the United States, the general trend is very similar.

Concentration of ownership has made it easier to introduce more efficient management methods, pooled resources, and, above all, new technologies able to speed up production, trim personnel, and, as a consequence, reduce spiraling costs. Here again, these technologies have been introduced at different times in each of the three countries under study. The most significant changes have been those associated with the computerization of newsroom and printshop procedures, but there have been other major innovations such as improved graphics capabilities and satellite printing plants.

NEW TECHNOLOGY

American newspaper publishers succeeded in bringing computerized technology to their operations much earlier than their European counterparts. The *Oklahoma City Times* and the *Oklahoma City Oklahoman* in 1963 became the first newspapers in the United States to process their entire news content by computer. They were followed by the *Wall Street Journal*, the *Los Angeles Times*, the *West Palm Beach Post Times*, and the *South Bend Tribune*.[28] However, while OCRs (optical character readers) became widespread very quickly, many smaller newspapers did not adopt VDTs (video display terminals) until the mid–1970s.[29]

In Britain, the electronic revolution began in the provinces in the 1970s with such newspapers as the *Western Morning News* in Plymouth and the *Eastern Daily Press* in Norwich. In the absence of such sophisticated systems as Atex in the United States, British provincial newspapers have developed electronic news editing systems in a very piecemeal manner. For economic reasons, some newspapers, like the *East Anglian Daily Times* in Ipswich, have built hybrid systems involving PCs that are used off-line for writing and editing, and switched on-line for input. The *Eastern Daily Press*, which in 1986 was one of the first to become fully automated, has developed its own software in conjunction with IBM.

These technological developments in provincial newspapers have taken a number of years to achieve because of resistance from the print unions. In London, the unions were notoriously militant and powerful until Robert Maxwell faced them down in a series of confrontations in the early and mid–1980s, and until Rupert Murdoch decided to move all his titles to a modern plant in London's dockland in early 1986. The decentralization of Fleet Street from the West End to lower-rent areas on London's fringes has made it possible to take advantage of new, computerized technology and smaller staffs, thus further weakening the grip of the print unions.[30] Now it is a matter of time until all the London dailies go to fully automated direct input.[31]

In the United States, conflict between management and the labor unions came to a head several years earlier. In the mid–1970s, the Newspaper and Graphic Communication Union threatened or initiated strike actions at a number of newspapers when publishers announced their decision to introduce new technologies. The most dramatic dispute occurred at the *Washington Post* in October 1975 when striking print workers vandalized presses, causing more than $3 million worth of damage. Management moved quickly to have the newspaper printed at nonunion plants outside the Washington area. Finally, after weeks of negotiation, the newspaper dismissed the entire press room crew and replaced them with nonunion workers.[32]

In France, the national print workers union (FFTL) is tremendously strong because it includes not only printers but almost every other category of worker, with the exception of journalists, involved in the production and delivery of newspapers. For this reason, only about twenty out of a total of eighty-five French dailies, either in Paris or the provinces, have begun to use any kind of electronic news processing system. To date, none has been able to negotiate a fully integrated single-key system with the union. Several have succeeded in introducing direct input from their branch offices, but, at headquarters, double keying is still in force.[33]

In France, too, there is also a degree of resistance from journalists who, as has already been pointed out, often think of themselves as literary intellectuals who take a perverse pride in not knowing how to use a typewriter, let alone a sophisticated piece of electronic equipment. For example, *Presse-Océan* in Nantes has a system of VDTs that would enable journalists to edit agency copy on screen, but journalists still have small dot matrix printers on their desks so that they can edit stories on hard copy.

It can be seen, therefore, that the introduction of new technology is governed by many factors, not only managerial decision and capitalization, but also availability, union approval and journalistic traditions. These various factors explain why newspaper technology is emerging at different speeds in France, Britain and the United States. However, there is no doubt that ownership in those countries, and this is particularly true for group ownership, has viewed new technology as an effective means of combating competition both from other newspapers and from other media.

It is impossible yet to say how successful newspapers will be at fighting competition from the so-called "new" media: cable television, home video, videotex, teletext, electronic newspapers, satellite broadcasting and other means of transborder information flow. As in the past, newspaper chains have bought their way into the new competition, thus confirming the trend toward multimedia "communication groups." Most American media groups now own interests in cable television and electronic publishing, but, so far, the other new media, with the possible exception of local teletext and home video, have not posed much of a threat. In Europe transborder television is already a reality and has been the subject of much intergovernmental concern. In Britain and France, videotex and teletext were once perceived as a real danger by media groups, but initial worries about them have been allayed by relatively slow public acceptance and an unwillingness to invest in their future development.[34]

Whatever new developments occur, on either side of the Atlantic, multimedia communications groups will no doubt continue to monitor them closely and take steps to absorb, or enter, any ventures likely to pose a threat. Gannett's new offering, "USA Today: The Television Show," which began on September 12, 1988, is a perfect example of how media groups may deal with new challenges. This program takes a brash newspaper whose bite-size information capsules are centered round a television culture and puts it on prime-time cable, thus combining newspaper, television and magazine into a kind of animated teletext with live performers.

AUDIENCE FRAGMENTATION

Perhaps the biggest challenge facing communications groups today is the demassification of the media and the fragmentation of audiences. These phenomena, brought about by changing lifestyles as well as the multiplication of media channels, are at different stages of development in the United States, France and Britain. Cable television, which has the strongest potential for fragmenting audiences, is now well developed in the United States, but remains embryonic in France and Britain. Both European countries, however, have ambitious cabling policies. The present network in France, covering only 3 percent of households, has a capacity of fifteen channels, but the number of transmitted programs varies from three to twelve. British networks, which cover 13 percent of households, are of lower capacity, four to six channels, distributing mainly national programs.[35] The development of cable television in these two countries is likely to be slow, probably not more than 10 percent per year, but certain. Meanwhile, more fundamental audience fragmentation has come from the multiplication of national television channels.

Changing lifestyles have also affected media usage. Television has become more popular in all three countries, and newspaper readership is down, although less so in Britain and France than in the United States. People are also more mobile, both socially and geographically, and spend more time on leisure activities, all of which tends to break down media usage patterns. Individual media vehicles, or groups owning only one kind of media, are less able to appeal to composite audiences, and, as a result, are finding it more difficult to attract advertising. The new communications groups, on the other hand, are able to reach diversified audiences across larger geographic areas via various combinations of media, and are therefore able to offer comprehensive advertising packages. The financial strength of these groups also enables them to buy the technology that can now tailor targeted editions for very specific audiences.

In summary, since World War II a number of changes have occurred affecting the ownership, management, staffing and editorial policies of news organizations. Although changes have taken place at different times and in different circumstances in France, Britain and the United States, the results have been largely the same.

With regard to newspapers, particularly regional newspapers, two parallel trends have emerged. The first is the need to satisfy the requirements of local audiences, which, according to editors in all three countries, are becoming increasingly interested in very local events and institutions, perhaps because of the impersonal, generic nature of the national media. The new technology brought in by multimedia communications groups now makes it possible to reach these different audiences with very specific targeted editions.

The second trend, which is the result of reduced personnel and increased newsholes imposed by new management policies, is a growing dependence on routine electronic news sources. Electronic news management systems, introduced by profit-conscious proprietors, encourage the greater use of standard agency copy for foreign and national news. Even where electronic systems have not yet been fully developed, as in certain French newspapers, time constraints prevent journalists from rewriting or even seriously editing raw agency dispatches.

The final outcome of all these changes is the growing homogenization of news content and editorial styles. Such homogenization, particularly with regard to national and international news, is no longer restricted to media systems in individual countries. It is now common across many Western economies. The particular focus of the present study, however, is foreign news. The next three chapters present evidence showing that foreign news coverage in regional newspapers in France, Britain and the United States is now almost identical.

NOTES

1. Albert and Terrou, *Histoire de la presse*, pp. 105–110.

2. James Curran and Jean Seaton, *Power Without Responsibility: The Press and Broadcasting in Britain*, 2d ed. (London: Methuen, 1985), pp. 75–90.

3. George T. Kurian (ed.), *World Press Encyclopedia* (New York: Facts on File, 1982), p. 948.

4. American Newspaper Publishers Association, *Facts about Newspapers '88* (Dulles Airport, Washington, D.C.: ANPA, April 1988).

5. Kurian, *World Press Encyclopedia*, p. 950.

6. Philip Weiss, "Invasion of the Gannettoids," *The New Republic* (February 1, 1987), p. 18.

7. This information comes from a fact sheet issued by *USA Today* and dated April 29, 1988.

8. Much of the information in this section comes from an industry-wide report prepared by Stuart Garner, editor-in-chief of Eastern Counties Newspapers, a family owned group in Britain that controls some forty titles, mainly weeklies, but also some successful dailies, all in the provinces.

9. Much of the information on the French provincial press comes from interviews with Louis Guéry, former director of the Centre de Formation des Journalistes in Paris, and author of *Quotidien régional: mon journal* (Paris: CFPJ-ARPEJ, 1987).

10. For general background on the French provincial press see the following: Mathien, *La presse quotidienne régionale*; Archambault and Lemoîne, *Quatre milliards de journaux*; Besson, *La presse locale en liberté surveillée*.

11. For general background on the British provincial press see the following: Simpson, *The Commercialization of the Regional Press*; Jackson, *The Provincial Press and the Community*; Clark, *Sixteen Million Readers: Evening Newspapers in the U.K.*

12. Alexander MacLeod, "New Technology, Avid Readers Kindle Renaissance for British Papers," *Christian Science Monitor*, November 20, 1988, p. 12.

13. Peter Dreier and Steve Weinberg, "Interlocking Directorates," *Columbia Journalism Review* (November-December 1979), pp. 51–68.

14. Ben Bagdikian, *The Media Monopoly*, 2d ed. (Boston: Beacon Press, 1987).

15. Mark Hollingsworth, *The Press and Political Dissent: A Question of Censorship* (London: Pluto Press, 1986), pp. 309–311.

16. Steve Lohr, "Britain's Maverick Mogul," *The New York Times Magazine* (May 1, 1988), p. 52 et seq.

17. Bernard Guillou, *Les groupes multimédias de communication* (Paris: La Documentation Française, 1984).

18. Patrice Lestroha, "Les gros poissons, la friture et les requins," *L'Evénement du jeudi* (January 21–27, 1988), pp. 8–10.

19. Balle, "The Communication Revolution and Freedom of Expression Redefined," p. 86.

20. Bill Powell, "Murdoch's Empire," *Newsweek* (August 22, 1988), pp. 42–43.

21. Lohr, "Britain's Maverick Mogul."

22. Albert and Terrou, *Histoire de la presse*, pp. 60–71.

23. Emery and Emery, *The Press and America*, pp. 373–380.

24. Albert and Terrou, *Histoire de la presse*, pp. 81–82.

25. MacLeod, "New Technology."

26. Hynds, *American Newspapers in the 1980s*, p. 81.

27. Nadine Toussaint (ed.), "La presse quotidienne," *Les Cahiers Français* No. 78 (October-December, 1976).

28. Hynds, *American Newspapers*, p. 86.

29. Interview with Paul McAuliffe, managing editor of the Evansville *Courier*.

30. MacLeod, "New Technology."

31. Lohr, "Britain's Maverick Mogul."

32. From reports in the *New York Times* throughout October, November and December, 1975.

33. Interview with Michel Poinot, president of the French Association of Provincial Newspaper Editors.

34. Gianpetro Mazzoleni, "Mass Telematics: Facts and Fiction," in Denis McQuail and Karen Siune, *New Media Politics: Comparative Per-*

spectives in Western Europe (London: Sage Publications, 1986), pp. 100–114.

35. Kees Brants, "Policing the Cable," in McQuail and Siune, *New Media Politics*, pp. 55–56.

PART II

JOURNALISTIC CHOICES

5

HOW THE STUDY WAS DONE

Previous chapters have shown that there are different journal-istic traditions and images in France, Britain and the United States, and one could expect them to produce different kinds of journalism. However, while journalistic styles and approaches may differ, actual news content appears to be very similar. Is this similarity real or only apparent? If it is real, why does such similarity exist when journalistic images are so divergent? These are questions that Part II of this study attempts to answer.

Answering these questions poses a number of problems, in particular what needs to be measured, and, then, how to meas-ure it. From the outset, it seemed obvious that systematic content analysis would be the only satisfactory method of measuring differences in news coverage. As to *what* was to be measured, it was decided that foreign news would be a better indicator of differences than national news, which might be strongly influ-enced by specific domestic issues and situations. Regional news-papers were selected for analysis in each of the three countries for reasons that will be explained below.

Content analysis can show the result of editorial decisions, but it cannot show the reasons behind them. This is why a survey questionnaire was given to journalists responsible for the selec-tion of foreign news in several regional newspapers in each country. The journalists were asked to rank a number of qualities they would look for when choosing a news item from a wire service, as well as some of the factors likely to influence their decision. At the same time, to identify some of the organizational or professional constraints guiding editorial choices, lengthy observation periods were spent in the newsrooms of three regional newspapers, one in each country. Finally, briefer visits were made to three other newspapers in each country. This chapter describes how these various research procedures were organized and conducted.

NEWSPAPER SELECTION

Regional newspapers were selected for analysis and observation rather than national newspapers for three specific reasons. First, there are no equivalent national newspapers in France, Britain and the United States, so there is no true basis for comparison. Most of the London morning newspapers still enjoy large circulations and national distribution. Only two or three of the Paris dailies can claim any kind of readership outside of the Paris area, and even then it is limited. In the United States, there are no truly national newspapers although Gannett's *USA Today* is attempting to establish national readership.

Second, it was felt that journalists in regional newspapers are less subject to some of the commercial pressures that exist in national news organizations and are more likely, therefore, to take editorial decisions for purely journalistic reasons rather than for reasons colored by considerations of profitability. On the whole, regional newspapers no longer have to face direct competition from other newspapers in their primary markets. Competition is usually limited to minor skirmishes on the periphery of their circulation areas. Furthermore, because of the nature of local journalism, regional journalists are much closer to their audiences and, as a result, are likely to be influenced more by their readers than by their professional peers or editorial superiors. In a sense, therefore, they are more representative of their national culture than are journalists working for national media.

Finally, regional newspapers were chosen rather than national newspapers because they are an underresearched area. A great

deal has been written about television and the big prestige newspapers, but regional newspapers have been sadly neglected,
from a research viewpoint, particularly in the United States. And
yet, as has been pointed out above, they are probably much
more in tune with the realities of everyday life and a genuine
national culture than are larger newspapers, which tend to reflect a synthetic, metropolitan, television-generated culture.

Individual regional newspapers were selected for study with
a great deal of care. It was felt that, if the study was to have
any significance, they should be as similar as possible. In fact,
a whole summer was spent visiting and interviewing newspaper
editors so as to make sure that the publications selected met a
number of specific criteria. The three newspapers selected for
individual study were the *Eastern Daily Press* in Norwich, Britain;
Le Courier de l'Ouest in Angers, France; and the *Courier* in Evansville, Indiana.

These newspapers have relatively similar circulations, taking
into account comparative readership levels in the three countries. Their circulation areas have approximately the same population base. They all have a strong regional focus, serving not
only the town in which they are published but also the surrounding counties. Beyond these general considerations, they
all find themselves in a monopoly or single-ownership situation,
which rules out extreme competition likely to affect editorial
decisions. Finally, they are all free of strong ideological leanings,
a factor that is particularly important in Europe where partisan
bias can seriously influence news content.

OBSERVATION

Two-week periods of observation were spent in each of the
three newspapers selected: May 25 to June 5, 1987, at *Le Courier
de l'Ouest*; June 15 to June 26, 1987, at the *Eastern Daily Press*;
and May 23 to June 3, 1988, at the Evansville *Courier*. Briefer
visits were made to the following newspapers:

The *Courier-Journal* in Louisville, Kentucky

The *Indianapolis Star* in Indianapolis, Indiana

The *Herald-Telephone** in Bloomington, Indiana

The *Yorkshire Post* in Leeds, Britain

The *East Anglian Daily Times* in Ipswich, Britain

The *Western Morning News* in Plymouth, Britain

Le Maine Libre in Le Mans, France

Presse-Océan in Nantes, France

Ouest-France in Rennes, France

Visits to these newspapers usually took the form of an interview with the editor or managing editor combined with a quick tour of the newsroom and technical facilities. The purpose of these visits was to gain added perspective and to make sure that what was observed in each of the three main newspapers was typical of practices and procedures in that particular country. Care was taken to select newspapers that were relatively dissimilar in size and prestige. For example, The *Courier-Journal*, The *Yorkshire Post* and *Ouest-France* are all larger, prestige newspapers, while The *Herald-Telephone*, The *Western Morning News* and *Le Maine Libre* are all smaller, relatively obscure publications outside of their circulation areas. The other three were selected for reasons of proximity or accessibility.

Two weeks were spent at each of the three main newspapers during which the researcher sat in on editorial conferences, interviewed senior editorial staff, and worked alongside those journalists responsible for the selection of foreign news. Below is a brief description of some of the chief characteristics of these three newspapers.

THE EVANSVILLE *COURIER*

Evansville, which is situated in the southwestern corner of Indiana, has a population of about 135,000 and is an important commercial center for surrounding rural areas. Its morning newspaper, the *Courier*, is distributed throughout a Standard Metropolitan Statistical Area of about 250,000, including counties

*The *Herald-Telephone* changed its name to the *Herald-Times* in May 1989.

in Kentucky across the Ohio River. The newspaper is owned by
Scripps-Howard. Its editor is president of the Courier Company,
which prints not only the *Courier* but also the city's evening
paper, the *Press*. On the edges of its circulation area the *Courier*
is in competition with the Louisville *Courier Journal*, the Hen-
derson *Gleaner*, the Bedford *Times-Mail*, and the Owensboro
Messenger-Inquirer. The *Courier* prints four editions, one each for
Kentucky, Indiana and Illinois, and a metro edition. Its total
daily circulation is around 64,000.

The newspaper is run on a day-to-day basis by a managing
editor with the help of four assistant managing editors, one each
for design/photography, metro, news and features/sport. The
assistant managing editor for news also acts as chief of the copy
desk and is assisted by a news editor. The *Courier* employs about
seventy journalists, but that figure also includes those who work
on the Sunday edition, which has a circulation of 117,000. The
newspaper takes the Associated Press, the NYT wire and the
Scripps-Howard News Service, which includes a number of syndicated columns. Other features are bought in as required. The
newspaper has one full-time correspondent in Washington,
housed in the Scripps-Howard office, and a state capital correspondent in Indianapolis. It has no branch offices and very few
local correspondents.

The managing editor (ME) holds two editorial conferences
each day, one at 2 P.M. and the other at 5 P.M. Both meetings,
which are very informal, are attended by the news, metro, business and sports editors. The first meeting is a general review of
news budgets and a rapid discussion of possible lead stories for
each page or section. The ME usually offers suggestions or guid-
ance particularly for any local stories he thinks should be expanded. The second meeting confirms these choices and
finalizes page one, subject to late developments. After that, the
editors are pretty much on their own. The ME leaves around 8
P.M. and lock-up time for the first run is 11:15 P.M.

The newsroom of the *Courier* is a large open room with work
stations grouped according to the different desks: metro, business, sports, features and copy desk, as well as the graphics
department. On most nights, the copy desk is staffed by the
AME for news, who functions as slotman; the news editor, who

functions as the wire editor; and two to four other journalists depending on circumstances. When the AME is off, the news editor sits in the slot.

Foreign news is taken from the AP international wire and is usually handled by one of two journalists on the copy desk. Both have a college education and are veteran journalists with many years of experience on this and other newspapers. Typically, foreign news items will appear as world briefs on the left-hand side of page two, but if the story merits more than two or three short paragraphs it will be placed on page three. If it is important enough, it may be used as a page one lead. On average, the newspaper does not carry more than five or six foreign news stories.

Like many other medium-sized newspapers in the United States, the *Courier* became fully electronic in the mid–1970s, after using an optical character recognition system for a brief period during which the copy desk continued to edit on hard copy. It now has an integrated Atex system. Management is also experimenting with modular pagination, but most of the savings that can be realized in the composition room have already been made. The managing editor of the newspaper believes that technical changes have made it possible to do the job more quickly, but now journalists are performing tasks that used to be done by linotype and composition room personnel. Generally speaking, this managing editor claims, the quality of news stories has dropped because journalists now have to concentrate on such tasks as entering correct coding, checking words and proof-reading.

LE COURIER DE L'OUEST

This morning newspaper is published in the city of Angers, which has a population of about 135,000 and which lies at the center of a fairly prosperous agricultural and wine-growing area known as Anjou, in west-central France. *Le Courier de l'Ouest* is owned by the heirs of the old Amaury group, which controls, among other publications, the Paris daily *Le Parisien Libéré*, several successful sports papers including *L'Equipe*, as well as periodicals such as the popular women's magazine *Marie France*.

Le Courier de l'Ouest faces strong competition from *Ouest-France* to the north and west, and from *La Nouvelle République du Centre-Ouest* to the south. On the eastern edge of its readership area, it competes on a more friendly basis with *Le Maine Libre*, also owned by the same group.

Because of this competition and also because of its situation in the center of a mainly rural region, *Le Courier de l'Ouest* is very much concerned with local events. It produces seven different editions, and three-fourths of the sixty to seventy pages printed daily are devoted to local, departmental or regional events. This detailed local coverage is provided by thirteen branch offices and a network of almost a thousand local correspondents, most of whom are unpaid or remunerated with free subscriptions. Total circulation is in the region of 105,000.

The newspaper is run on a daily basis by a managing editor (directeur de la rédaction), a news editor (rédacteur en chef), and a senior layout and technical director (secrétaire général de rédaction). They are assisted by seven local page editors (secrétaires de rédaction), one for each edition and a page-one editor who also acts as wire editor and coordinates general and foreign news. All in all, *Le Courier de L'Ouest* employs some seventy-five journalists either in the central newsroom or in the branch offices. The newspaper takes Agence France Presse and the French service of the Associated Press. It has no Paris office, but it regularly uses the services of a Paris-based syndicated columnist who is well known and who, according to audience research, is appreciated by readers. The managing editor states that this columnist obviates the need for a bureau in the capital.

There is only one editorial conference, held at 6 P.M., by which time the local page editors and the page-one editor have a fairly good idea of what the newspaper will look like. Some of them will have consulted individually with the news editor during the course of the afternoon. The editorial conference is a rather structured meeting in which the senior layout director plays a major role. He is the person who establishes the number of pages that are available for the following day. One of the main functions of the meeting is to decide what stories will appear on the page-one summary. Each lead story is formally approved by the news editor. Foreign news is never discussed unless there is a major story from overseas that might deserve special attention. At the end of the meeting, the page editors leave, and the managing editor, the news editor, the senior layout editor and the page-one editor decide what will go on the front page. Although the news editor stays until 7:30 or 8 P.M., the newspaper is put to bed by the page editors who are also responsible for preliminary layout. The copy deadline for the first edition is 8:15 P.M.

As in many French newspapers, the layout of the newsroom at *Le Courier de l'Ouest* is far less open than in most British and American newspapers. There is a general area shared by the page editors and the sports desk, but most of the newspaper's reporters work in the branch offices so there is not the bustle usually associated with central newsrooms. The managing editor, the news editor and the senior layout director all have private offices, while the copy desk is situated in a separate room next to the wire printers. Because of the decentralized organization of the newspaper, the copy desk usually consists of the page-one editor/wire editor and two other journalists. Sometimes, only one other journalist is on duty.

The agency copy, which comes in on printers, is hand sorted by the page-one editor, who comes in early so as to have a selection of twelve to fifteen main stories ready for the 6 P.M. editorial conference. After the conference, by which time the rest of the copy desk has arrived, these and other minor stories are edited and laid out. Editing is done with a pencil and generally consists in shortening agency dispatches. Very little, if any, rewriting is done but copy editors all say they wish they had time to do more than just basic cutting and trimming. After editing, the copy is dispatched to the composition room by pneumatic tube.

Foreign news is selected by the page-one editor from either AFP or the French AP wire. There are two regular page-one editors, both highly experienced. One, who has been with the newspaper for thirty-two years, has no college education or formal journalism training. The other, a woman, has been a journalist for eleven years and is a graduate of the Strasbourg School of Journalism. Foreign news usually takes the form of eight to ten briefs on the left-hand side of one of the two "France/Monde" (France/World) pages. Bigger foreign stories may appear elsewhere on these pages, or on page one, with display heads and photographs. It is not uncommon for the newspaper to have as many as fifteen foreign news items.

Although the management of *Le Courier de l'Ouest* intends to install VDTs throughout the newspaper, during the period of observation all news handling and editing was done by hand, at least on the copy desk and in the central newsroom. However, even at that period, all the branch offices were equipped with screens and an agreement had been reached with the union that allowed direct input from these offices. Apart from union resistance, however, many of the page editors (secrétaires de rédaction) are somewhat reluctant to accept electronic systems, partly because they feel their personal prestige might be threatened, but also because the systems are not standardized. Copy-desk personnel view themselves as journalists and not technicians, but earn about 15 percent less than technical staff. If they are asked to perform what they consider to be a technical job, they may well want more money. Also, although many publications now seem to want to install Datox (the French version of Atex), there is still no standard system, and this creates problems of adaptation for journalists who wish to move to other newspapers.

Ultimately, the management of *Le Courier de l'Ouest* would like to decentralize all page editors, except the central copy desk, by sending them to the branch offices. Although these and other changes may be slow in coming, it is obvious that French journalistic traditions are rapidly disappearing and that, as commercial pressures build, French journalists are having to cope with many of the constraints already facing their British and American counterparts.

THE *EASTERN DAILY PRESS*

The *EDP*, as it is most often referred to, appears in the ancient cathedral city of Norwich, in southeastern England, which has a population of around 125,000. The county of Norfolk, in which Norwich is situated, was long considered a rural backwater, but in recent years, the construction of a new highway has put it within two hours of London and the area is now developing fast. The *EDP* was originally owned by three prominent Quaker families with strong liberal leanings. It now belongs to a private company, Eastern Counties Newspapers, the ownership of which is shared by representatives of two of the original families, the Colemans and the Copemans, and a large insurance company based in Norwich, the Norwich Union.

The company controls about twenty titles, including eleven weeklies and a number of freesheets, but also some other successful dailies including the local evening newspaper, the *Eastern Evening News*. It also has an interest in the *East Anglian Daily Times* located in Ipswich, about forty miles south of Norwich. It is interesting to note that the *Eastern Daily Press* and the *East Anglian Daily Times* are the only two morning newspapers in Britain to have increased their circulation in recent years, which says much for the group's management, although part of its success must be attributed to economic growth in its readership areas. The *EDP* has three editions, one for west Norfolk, one for south and east Norfolk, and a final edition for north Norfolk and the city. Total circulation is around 96,000. For geographic reasons, the *EDP*'s main competition comes from some of the East Midlands newspapers, in particular the *Peterborough Times*.

The management of the *EDP* appears to be somewhat top heavy but that is probably because all the newspapers in the group are run from the same building. The editor in chief is also responsible for other newspapers and sits on the main board of Eastern Counties Newspapers. Although he takes an active interest in the *EDP*, his function is more that of publisher. Day-to-day management of the newspaper is provided by an editor and a managing editor, whose functions are somewhat different from what might be expected from their titles in the United States. The managing editor, who is a former editor of the newspaper, deals exclusively with administration, legal questions and personnel matters, including hiring and training. The editor, while dealing with editorials and columns, acts more like the managing editor of an American newspaper, except that he has no administrative responsibilities. Everyone concerned seems satisfied with this arrangement.

The assistant editor, who is the equivalent of assistant managing editor for news, acts as slotman, although there is no slot and rim as in the United States. In British terms, the assistant editor sits at the top table, sifts stories from the incoming wires and sends them down table to "subs" or sub editors with instructions regarding the type of treatment and editing required. He is responsible for the content and layout of pages one and two as well as world news. He is assisted down table by four or five subs who may also do local news. A chief sub does the layout of inside pages, while a "copy taster" sifts incoming local news. On any given evening, there are probably about 12 journalists working in the *EDP* newsroom, although, all in all, the newspaper employs about 150 journalists on its two dailies and its various weeklies.

The *EDP* takes the Press Association wire, which is a mix of Reuters and the AP world service. The newspaper has a three-man London office covering Parliament, labor issues and foreign affairs. It also has eleven district offices located in smaller towns throughout its circulation area. Each of these district offices produces a weekly and files local news to head office. The company also relies on about 300 "parish pump" correspondents who supply information about village fetes, Red Cross fundraisers, cricket matches and other local events. Most of this information is used in the weeklies, but some of it finds its way into the *EDP*.

The editor holds one editorial conference at 4:30 P.M. attended by the deputy editor, the news editor and the heads of the various desks. The main focus of the meeting is local news and a discussion of possible "splash stories," or page-one leads. National and world news is not reviewed at this time, mainly because the night editor (the assistant editor) does not come in until around 5:30 P.M. after the Press Association night lead schedule has dropped. However, during the early part of the evening, the editor spends a lot of time on the newsroom floor and consults frequently with the assistant editor as he makes a first sift of national and international news. The deadline for the first edition is 12:30 A.M.

Foreign news coverage consists of seven or eight world NIBs (News in Brief) in the left-hand column of page three, as well as more important stories on page two, or even page one if the story is big enough. The newspaper usually carries eleven or twelve foreign news items. The assistant editor usually starts with the page-three world briefs because they can be easily edited and are unlikely to change. The other foreign news stories can usually be finished early,too, except for late news out of the United States. The assistant editor is a seventeen-year veteran who took journalism courses but never went to college. The chief sub, who replaces him on his nights off, never took journalism courses but has a university degree.

The *EDP* was one of the first British newspapers to adopt electronic news management. It went to full screens in 1986 and is now fully automated. In conjunction with IBM, it has developed its own software called ECNews. According to the editor, it is now possible to get a finished bromo (stereotype) from a print command without further intervention from the typesetters.

The above description of the three main newspapers observed is intended to provide a general context for the rest of the study and is limited to facilities, staffing and newsroom procedures. A more detailed discussion of the criteria governing editorial choices will be given in the next chapter.

SURVEY

At all the newspapers visited, those journalists responsible for the selection of foreign news were asked to fill out a self-administered survey questionnaire, a copy of which is appended to the methodological note at the end of this study. Among other things, these twenty-three journalists were asked to identify qualities sought when selecting a news item from a wire service. They were given the following list to choose from:

- Accuracy
- How topical
- Local impact
- Right length
- Human interest
- Byline (author)

- Geographic origin
- Other

The journalists were also asked to rank these qualities in order of importance. They were then asked to repeat the same operation for *foreign* news items.

Finally, they were asked to identify and rank factors guiding the selection of news. They were again given a list to choose from:

- General editorial policy
- Professional training
- Immediate supervisor
- Fellow journalists
- Personal convictions
- Readers' interest
- Other

Obviously, the responses to these questions are self-reported and may not accurately reflect what individual journalists think, or believe they think, about this particular aspect of their work. They are, therefore, subject to caution. However, taken together, they do give some indication of the relative perceived importance of certain criteria used in the selection of news items from a wire service. The results of this survey are reported in the next chapter.

CONTENT ANALYSIS

Systematic content analysis was used to compare foreign news coverage of the three main newspapers, the *Eastern Daily Press*, the Evansville *Courier* and *Le Courier de l'Ouest* for the two-week period from May 4 to May 15, 1987. The wire services taken by the newspapers were also analyzed for the same period. These were the Agence France Press and the French service of the AP in France, the Press Association in Britain, and the AP in the United States.

All foreign news items with a foreign dateline moved by the

wire services or printed by the newspapers were analyzed in a number of ways. They were coded for origin, that is, whether the action reported took place in a country of the northern hemisphere or the southern hemisphere. They were also coded as violent or nonviolent. Finally, they were placed in one of thirty-three different subject categories, shown in Table 2. In all 2,727 news items were coded.

The foreign news items appearing in the three newspapers

Table 2
Subject Categories Used in Content Analysis

```
 1. Diplomatic/political
 2. Internal political conflict
 3. Elections, campaigns
 4. Other political matters or legislation
 5. Armed conflict or the threat of armed conflict
 6. Peace moves, negotiations
 7. Military expenditure, arms deals
 8. Trade agreements
 9. International trade, import/export
10. Economic performance
11. Prices, cost of living
12. Industrial projects
13. Agricultural matters
14. Industrial disputes
15. Monetary and exchange
16. Energy
17. Disaster/famine relief
18. Military aid
19. Other aid
20. Social problems
21. Crime, police matters
22. Air crashes, accidents
23. Culture, arts
24. Religion
25. Scientific/medical
26. Entertainment
27. Sport
28. Human interest/bizarre
29. Civil unrest
30. Environment/pollution
31. Natural disasters
32. Terrorism
33. Other
```

```
     A detailed explanation of coding categories, and a
discussion of intercoder reliability are to be found in the
methodological note at the end of this study.
```

were also coded for prominence on a scale of one to five. They were given one point for each of the following:

- Front-page location
- Front-page location above the fold
- More than three paragraphs
- Printed with photograph
- Printed across two or more columns

The detailed results of this content analyis are reported in the next chapter.

NEWS PROFILE

In order to give extra context to the study, the following news profile for the period analyzed (May 4 to May 15, 1987) was prepared from reports in the *Times* of London, the *New York Times* and *Le Monde*.

During the first week, it could not be said that any particular event dominated the news, but a number of major stories received almost daily coverage. Interest in the Iran-contra affair grew as congressional hearings got under way in Washington. General Secord's testimony was given extensive coverage. Still in the United States, Gary Hart's misfortunes and his decision to withdraw from the presidential race also received heavy coverage. Finally, toward the end of the week, CIA director William Casey died.

In the Middle East, the Israeli cabinet was split over the issue of a peace conference. Arafat's attempts to offer an olive branch seemed only to inflame the crisis in the Israeli government. Meanwhile, Israeli jets bombed a Palestinian camp in Sidon two days in a row. Also in the Middle East, the prime minister of Lebanon resigned.

In Europe, Britain was gripped by election fever as Prime Minister Thatcher announced a general election on June 11. The Tories seemed poised for a resounding victory. West German government officials expressed serious doubts about the acceptability of the Soviet zero-option arms proposal. In Lyons,

France, preparations got under way for the trial of Nazi war criminal Klaus Barbie. Jury selection proved to be very difficult as numerous jurors bowed out. In Austria, Kurt Waldheim continued to face accusations that he had participated in Nazi activities during World War II.

Elsewhere in the world, South African elections were held in a climate of protest and controversy. Students were arrested by the police, and black voters stayed at home. Results showed a surge of the far right. Elections were also held in Malta and Italy.

Finally, on a lighter note, this was the week of the Trash Barge, the *Break of Dawn*, which continued to seek a home for its unwanted cargo.

During the second week, interest in the Iran-contra hearings continued unabated as former security adviser Robert McFarlane testified on Capitol Hill and the involvement of the Sultan of Brunei was revealed. President Reagan denied that the affair had dealt him a "mortal wound." William Casey was buried, along with a store of secrets, it was felt, and Governor Michael Dukakis of Massachusetts was tipped to replace Gary Hart as Democratic front-runner in the presidential race.

In the Middle East, there were more Israeli raids in Lebanon. The Israeli cabinet remained divided over the peace conference issue and, by Thursday, the Peres cabinet was reported to have failed. In Europe, the Barbie trial got under way in Lyons, France, but, later during the week, Barbie refused to appear at any more of the hearings. Bonn continued to remain undecided over the zero-arms option, and this was viewed as an obstacle to Secretary of State George Schultz's efforts to reach a missile agreement in Europe.

Meanwhile, in other parts of the world, the first democratic elections in sixteen years were held in the Philippines. Indian Prime Minister Gandhi bolstered forces in the Punjab as Sikh trouble flared again. There were serious student riots in South Korea, and, in China, forest fires devastated huge areas in the northeast of the country. At the end of the week, the government of Fiji fell after a military coup. There were fears that this would be followed by more takeovers in small nations in the Pacific and the Caribbean.

Finally, in the world of entertainment, all the newspapers reported the death of actress Rita Hayworth.

It is interesting to note certain geographic, ethnic and political biases even in such prestigious newspapers as the *Times* of London, the *New York Times* and *Le Monde*. For reasons that seem quite normal and acceptable given Britain's colonial past, the *Times* tends to give more coverage to South Africa, India, Malta and certain areas of Asia. In the same way, for partly strategic and partly ethnic reasons, the *New York Times* devotes more space to Israel, Italy, Central America, Afghanistan and Jewish affairs, particularly in the Soviet Union. *Le Monde*, too, concentrates on former or existing French overseas possessions, such as Vietnam, Algiers, Morocco and New Caledonia, and, possibly for ideological reasons, it also provides extensive analysis of political issues in Turkey, China and Brazil.

Such bias is just one of the criteria governing the selection of foreign news. This and other criteria identified from the observation, content analysis and survey described above will be discussed in detail in the next chapter.

6

FINDINGS

This chapter reports the results of the research procedures described in Chapter 5. First, content analysis shows what kind of
foreign news coverage is provided by the three newspapers studied, as well as by the wire services to which they subscribe. It
establishes the proportions that exist between various subject
categories in each media vehicle, and it also indicates the prominence given to these subject categories by each newspaper.
Then, an analysis of survey responses shows how journalists
rank a number of criteria likely to guide their selection of news
items. Finally, a discussion of observational data collected during
field-work suggests a broader framework of influences affecting
foreign news coverage in regional newspapers.

CONTENT ANALYSIS

The results of the content analysis are most clearly shown in
table form. Generally speaking, the data presented in Tables 3
and 4 are remarkably homogeneous across the four news agencies and the three newspapers. There are a few results that
diverge somewhat from the overall norm, and these may be
explained perhaps by differences in the journalistic images and
traditions that continue to be prevalent in each country. However, it must be stressed that such divergences in the data are

Table 3
Foreign News Coverage by Subject Category

	Percentages of stories by news service				by newspaper			
	AFP	AP	FAP	PA	EC	EDP	CO	ALL
1. Diplomatic/political	18.5	10.9	10.1	9.5	8.6	9.2	12.2	13.0
2. Intern. pol.conflict	5.8	8.6	5.3	5.5	6.1	16.1	4.0	6.4
3. Elections, campaigns	6.2	7.1	5.7	4.6	7.4	6.2	9.7	6.0
4. Other pol. legisl.	3.6	4.3	3.1	3.8	8.7	3.9	1.6	3.7
5. Armed conflict	5.0	6.9	1.7	5.0	6.2	4.6	4.0	4.9
6. Peace moves, negtns.	4.8	6.0	3.7	3.6	0.0	1.5	0.8	4.0
7. Mil. expend., arms	3.6	4.9	2.1	3.2	2.5	1.5	1.6	3.2
8. Trade agreements	0.0	0.3	0.0	0.0	0.0	0.0	0.0	0.0
9. Int. trade, imp/exp.	1.6	1.1	1.5	1.3	1.2	1.5	0.0	1.4
10. Econ. performance	0.5	1.5	1.7	0.7	3.7	0.8	0.0	1.0
11. Prices, cost of liv.	0.1	0.6	0.6	0.0	0.0	0.0	0.8	0.3
12. Indust. projects	2.1	0.0	1.7	1.3	1.2	0.0	0.0	1.4
13. Agricul. matters	1.1	0.3	0.2	0.9	0.0	2.3	0.0	0.7
14. Indust. disputes	0.7	0.6	1.5	2.0	1.2	0.0	2.4	1.2
15. Monetary, exchange	0.5	2.3	2.0	0.0	0.0	0.0	0.8	0.9
16. Energy	0.1	0.3	0.8	0.7	1.2	0.0	0.0	0.3
17. Disast./fam. relief	0.1	0.0	0.4	0.0	0.0	0.0	0.0	0.1
18. Military aid	0.4	0.3	0.0	0.5	0.0	0.0	0.0	0.3
19. Other aid	0.5	0.0	0.8	0.2	0.0	0.8	0.0	0.4
20. Social problems	4.7	5.1	5.5	2.6	3.7	0.0	3.3	4.1
21. Crime, police	7.8	8.3	9.1	11.3	15.9	15.2	13.0	9.7
22. Air crashes, accid.	2.8	3.2	3.8	6.6	2.4	3.9	4.9	4.0
23. Culture, arts	2.8	5.4	5.3	6.1	7.4	4.6	3.3	4.6
24. Religion	2.3	2.3	1.3	1.6	1.2	2.3	2.4	1.9
25. Scientif., medical	6.1	2.6	9.0	5.2	1.2	3.9	8.9	5.9
26. Entertainment	1.1	0.6	1.3	2.9	2.5	3.8	3.3	1.7
27. Sport	0.2	0.3	2.3	1.5	0.0	3.1	0.0	1.0
28. Human int., bizarre	2.8	2.3	2.8	4.3	2.4	2.3	10.5	3.3
29. Civil unrest	6.5	5.5	4.3	5.8	3.6	3.1	6.5	5.5
30. Environ./pollution	1.6	1.7	4.2	2.1	0.0	2.3	2.4	2.3
31. Natural disasters	0.9	2.9	1.5	2.8	6.2	2.3	2.4	1.9
32. Terrorism	4.2	4.3	4.9	4.7	4.9	4.6	0.8	4.4
33. Other	0.6	0.0	0.6	0.0	0.0	0.8	0.0	0.4
No. of foreign news items	938	350	545	559	81	131	123	2727

AFP = Agence France Presse   EC = Evansville Courier
AP = Associated Press   EDP = Eastern Daily Press
FAP = French Service of AP   CO = Courier de l'Ouest
PA = Press Association   ALL = All media together

minor. This is borne out by a systematic analysis of the data comparing agency to agency, newspaper to newspaper, and newspaper to agency.

Agency to Agency

The overall subject category percentages given in Table 3 show three divergences that are relatively significant. In Category 1,

AFP is seen to devote 18.5 percent of its foreign news coverage to diplomatic and political affairs, compared with 10.9 percent for AP, 10.1 percent for AP's French service, and 9.5 percent for the Press Association. This may be because AFP views itself as an official agency of record and therefore feels obliged to keep closer track of intergovernmental affairs than do the other agencies.[1] This interest in diplomatic and political affairs is further echoed by one of the agency's clients, *Le Courier de l'Ouest*, which gives slightly more attention to this category of foreign news than do the British and American newspapers.

In Category 5, the French service of AP shows only 1.7 percent of its foreign coverage devoted to armed conflict, or the threat of armed conflict, as against 5 percent for AFP, 6.9 percent for AP, and 5 percent for PA. This may be explained by the fact that AP's French service seeks to complement the official French news agency and, presumably, considers that there is no point in duplicating this kind of coverage.[2] This enables it to devote more space to other subject categories such as Category 25, in which its foreign coverage of scientific and medical matters reaches 9 percent, compared to AFP's 6.1 percent, PA's 5.2 percent, and AP's low 2.6 percent.

Some of these differences are perhaps even more apparent in Table 4. In collapsed categories 1 to 4, AFP is seen to devote considerably more coverage to political matters than either PA or AP's French service. Similarly, in collapsed categories 5 to 7, AP's French service devotes considerably less coverage to hostilities than any of the other agencies.

Other minor divergences occur in Category 20 (social problems), in which PA has less coverage than the other three; in Category 22 (air crashes and accidents), in which PA has more coverage than the others; in Category 23 (culture and the arts), in which AFP has less coverage than the others; and in Category 30 (environment and pollution), in which AP's French service has more coverage than the others.

Newspaper to Newspaper

On the whole, there is more divergence among the newspapers than the news agencies. This is logical if one considers that

Table 4
Foreign News Coverage—Main Subject Categories

Percentages

	AFP	AP	FAP	PA	EC	EDP	CO	ALL
Political (1-4)*	34.1	30.9	24.2	23.4	30.8	34.5	27.5	29.1
Hostilities (5-7)*	13.4	17.8	7.5	11.8	8.7	7.6	6.4	12.1
Economy (8-16)*	6.7	7.0	10.0	6.9	8.5	4.6	4.0	7.2
Social problems	4.7	5.1	5.5	2.6	3.7	0.0	3.3	4.1
Crime and police	7.8	8.3	9.1	11.3	15.9	15.2	13.0	9.7
Crashes, accidents	2.8	3.2	3.8	6.6	2.4	3.0	4.9	4.0
Culture	2.8	5.4	5.3	6.1	7.4	4.6	3.3	4.6
Scientific/medical	6.1	2.6	9.0	5.2	1.2	3.9	8.9	5.9
Human int., bizarre	2.8	2.3	2.8	4.3	2.4	2.3	10.5	3.3
Civil unrest	6.5	5.5	4.3	5.8	3.6	3.1	6.5	5.5
Terrorism	4.2	4.3	4.9	4.7	4.9	4.6	0.8	4.4
Natural disasters	0.9	2.9	1.5	2.8	6.2	2.3	2.4	1.9
No. of news items	861	333	479	511	77	112	112	2503

* These aggregate categories were obtained by collapsing the
individual categories (shown in parentheses) from the previous
table.

AFP = Agence France Presse   EC = Evansville Courier
AP = Associated Press   EDP = Eastern Daily Press
FAP = French service of AP   CO = Courier de l'Ouest
PA = Press Assocation   ALL = All media together

press agencies have to serve a large number of subscribers, frequently with different cultural or ethnic affiliations, and are,
therefore, more inclined to produce a uniformly acceptable mix
of news than are regional newspapers which usually cater to a
well-defined audience sharing similar origins and lifestyles.

In Table 3, Category 2 shows that the *Eastern Daily Press* gives
far more coverage of internal political conflict than do the other
two newspapers. Indeed, the *EDP* devotes 16.1 percent of its
coverage to this category, as against 6.1 percent for the Evansville

Courier and 4 percent for *Le Courier de l'Ouest*. This is probably because all the events around the Iran-contra affair were coded as "internal political conflict." In view of the "special relationship" between Britain and the United States, British newspapers, even in the provinces, were far more likely to give greater coverage to these events than was *Le Courier de l'Ouest*, while of course, for the Evansville *Courier*, Irangate was domestic and not foreign news. This divergence is attenuated somewhat in the collapsed political categories 1 to 4 in Table 4.

Elsewhere in Table 3, it can be seen that the Evansville *Courier* demonstrates a stronger interest in other political affairs and legislation, in economic performance, culture and the arts and natural disasters, but provides no coverage of pollution or environmental matters. At the same time, the *Eastern Daily Press* focuses more on agricultural matters and sport than the other two newspapers, but appears to have no interest in social problems. *Le Courier de l'Ouest* gives more attention to industrial disputes, scientific and medical affairs, human interest stories and civil unrest, but has no coverage of international trade. Once again, however, it should be stressed that all these differences are relatively minor, the largest being a spread of only 7.7 percentage points in Category 25, which covers scientific and medical affairs.

Newspaper to Agency

The Evansville *Courier* and the Associated Press

The greatest divergence, although still relatively minor, is in Category 21 of Table 3 in which the Evansville *Courier* is seen to devote 15.9 percent of its foreign coverage to crime and police matters, while AP, from which it takes all its foreign news, shows a figure of only 8.3 percent. There are a few other even smaller divergences. The *Courier* gives slightly more emphasis than AP to other political matters and legislation, but devotes slightly less coverage to peace moves, monetary and exchange, and pollution and environmental matters.

The *Eastern Daily Press* and the Press Association

As has already been noted, the *EDP* devotes a substantial 16.1 percent of its coverage to internal political conflict, while PA gives only a meager 5.5 percent. This is surprising. It has been argued above that the *EDP* might be expected to provide more coverage than the other newspapers because of Irangate, but the fact that its coverage is more extensive than that of the wire service from which it takes its foreign news suggests that some other influence is at work here, possibly the individual preferences of the journalists selecting foreign news items. This is a point that will be discussed later in the section on observation.

Table 4 also shows that the newspaper pays more attention generally to political topics than does the news agency. Finally, in Table 3 it can be seen that the *EDP* gives no coverage to industrial projects, industrial disputes and social problems, while PA does provide some minimal coverage of these topics.

Le Courier de l'Ouest and Agence France Presse

The most obvious divergence, although again still relatively minor, is to be found in Category 28 of Table 3, which shows that the French newspaper devotes 10.5 percent of its foreign news coverage to human interest and bizarre stories, whereas AFP's coverage is no more than 2.8 percent, which, incidentally, is very similar to that of the other two newspapers and the other three agencies. Only *Le Courier* devotes so much attention to this topic, and it is not altogether clear why, although, for reasons that will be discussed later, it is possible to speculate that it is because of the personal idiosyncracies of the journalists involved in the selection of foreign news items.

There are other minor divergences, with *Le Courier* giving more coverage to crime and police matters, and AFP giving more coverage to diplomatic and political affairs, peace moves, industrial projects and terrorism.

Le Courier de l'Ouest and AP's French service

On the whole, there is probably slightly less divergence between *Le Courier de l'Ouest* and AP's French service than between *Le Courier* and AFP. Most instances of divergence occur in the same categories, for example crime and police matters, and human interest and bizarre, where the paper carries proportionately more coverage than the wire services.

Agence France Presse and AP's French Service

Differences between the two news agencies are very slight in the individual categories of Table 3. They are somewhat magnified, however, in Table 4, which shows AFP giving more coverage to political affairs and hostilities. But, even here, the largest spread is less than 10 percentage points.

All Newspapers and All Agencies Together

Generally speaking, the overall foreign news agenda of the newspapers faithfully mirrors that of the wire services. There is, however, one exception in Category 21 of Table 3, which shows coverage of crime and police matters. AFP, AP, AP's French service and PA show percentages of 7.8, 8.3, 9.1 and 11.3, respectively, while the percentages for the newspapers are consistently higher, with 15.9 percent for the Evansville *Courier*, 15.2 for the *Eastern Daily Press* and 13.0 percent for *Le Courier de l'Ouest*.

Although it is not possible to generalize, there seems to be at least a hint here that the editors of regional newspapers in the United States, Britain and France are more inclined to favor the relatively sensationalistic categories of crime and police matters than are the wire services from which they take their foreign news. Several influences capable of governing this inclination suggest themselves, including general editorial policy, personal idiosyncracies of journalists, and, more simply, the length and style of crime and police stories reported by the news agencies. More will be said about these in the discussion of criteria at the end of this chapter.

This conclusion is consistent with the findings of the Wilhoit and Weaver study, "Foreign News Coverage in Two U.S. News Services: An Update," which concludes, among other things, that local editors give more emphasis to violent stories from developing countries than do the wire services.[3]

Prominence

Various attempts have been made to measure the "play," or "attention" or "prominence" of news items, and some of them have proved to be satisfactory.[4] However, when dealing with the short foreign news items to be found in regional newspapers, existing scales are not accurate enough. The system used in this study takes into account the brevity of these news items by allocating one point to each of the following:

• Front-page location
• Front-page location above the fold
• More than three paragraphs
• Printed with a photograph or illustration
• Printed across two or more columns

Tables 5, 6, and 7 give prominence ratings for each of the newspapers analyzed. The ratings correspond to the following degrees of prominence:

1 = very little prominence
2 = moderate prominence
3 = significant prominence
4 = major prominence
5 = maximum prominence

Tables 5, 6 and 7 show *all* the foreign news items given one or more prominence rating points in each of the three newspapers. Whereas in previous tables the percentages of coverage devoted to various subject categories were seen, with a few exceptions, to be remarkably similar, the three prominence tables show some interesting differences.

The most obvious difference is the considerable prominence given to internal political conflict by the *Eastern Daily Press*. Out of a total of thirty-four news items given a prominence rating, fourteen, or 41 percent, are concerned with internal political conflict, as compared to 14.3 percent in the Evansville *Courier*, and only 5.9 percent in *Le Courier de l'Ouest*. Furthermore, news

Table 5
All Foreign News Items Given Prominence in the Evansville *Courier*
(total of 28)

Subject category of each story	Type	# Graphs	Rating
Diplomatic	S/NV	12	4
Intern. pol. conflict	N/NV	20	3
Crime and police	N/NV	14	3
Culture	N/NV	12	3
Culture	N/NV	10	3
Natural disaster	S/NV	9	3
Intern. pol. conflict	N/NV	20	2
Elections	S/NV	17	2
Intern. pol. conflict	S/NV	14	2
Civil unrest	S/V	13	2
Elections	N/NV	13	2
Culture	N/NV	13	2
Terrorism	S/NV	13	2
Energy	N/NV	12	2
Terrorism	S/NV	12	2
Military expenditure	N/NV	12	2
Elections	N/NV	11	2
Diplomatic/political	N/NV	8	2
Economic performance	N/NV	8	2
Culture	N/NV	7	2
Armed conflict	S/V	7	2
Social problems	N/NV	6	2
International trade	N/NV	5	2
Human interest	N/V	1	2
Military expenditure	N/NV	12	1
Diplomatic/political	S/NV	10	1
Industrial projects	N/NV	5	1
Intern. pol. conflict	N/NV	4	1

```
N  = news items originating in the northern hemisphere
S  = news items originating in the southern hemisphere
V  = news items involving violence
NV = news items not involving violence
```

Detailed definitions of these types of news item are given
in the methodological note at the end of the study.

items about internal political conflict are consistently given a
higher prominence rating in the *EDP* than in the other two
newspapers. They are also given more space, a total of 122 paragraphs, which is by far the largest amount of space given to
any subject category in any of the three newspapers. The next
most prominent categories in the *EDP* are crime and police mat-

Table 6

**All Foreign News Items Given Prominence in *Le Courier de l'Ouest*
(total of 34)**

Subject category of each story	Type	# Graphs	Rating
Diplomatic/political	N/NV	2	4
Religion	N/NV	8	3
Diplomatic/political	N/NV	7	3
Intern. pol. conflict	N/V	6	3
Diplomatic/political	N/NV	6	3
Elections	N/NV	6	3
Entertainment	N/NV	6	3
Elections	S/NV	5	3
Elections	N/NV	4	3
Diplomatic/political	N/NV	10	2
Crime and police	S/NV	9	2
Terrorism	S/NV	7	2
Diplomatic	N/NV	6	2
Military expenditure	N/NV	6	2
Natural disaster	S/NV	5	2
Crime and police	N/NV	5	2
Civil unrest	N/V	5	2
Elections	N/NV	4	2
Armed conflict	S/NV	6	1
Peace moves	S/NV	5	1
Elections	N/NV	5	1
Human interest	N/NV	4	1
Intern. pol. conflict	N/NV	4	1
Diplomatic/political	N/NV	4	1
Other political	N/NV	4	1
Crime and police	N/V	4	1
Diplomatic/political	N/NV	4	1
Crime and police	N/V	3	1
Civil unrest	N/NV	3	1
Armed conflict	S/V	3	1
Culture	S/NV	2	1
Elections	N/NV	2	1
Air crashes	N/NV	2	1
Industrial disputes	N/NV	2	1

```
N  = news items originating in the northern hemisphere
S  = news items originating in the southern hemisphere
V  = news items involving violence
NV = news items not involving violence
Detailed definitions are given in the methodological note.
```

ters, which account for 14.7 percent of the prominent news
items, and elections, which account for 8.8 percent.

The Evansville *Courier* also gives the most prominence to internal political conflict with fifty-eight paragraphs and 14.3 percent of all items allocated rating points. Culture comes next, also

Table 7
All Foreign News Items Given Prominence in the *Eastern Daily Press* (total of 34)

Subject category of each story	Type	# Graphs	Rating
Intern. pol. conflict	N/NV	17	4
Peace moves	N/NV	11	4
Other political	N/NV	14	3
Crime and police	N/NV	12	3
Intern. pol. conflict	N/NV	10	3
Civil unrest	N/V	10	3
Entertainment	N/NV	9	3
Intern. pol. conflict	N/NV	9	3
Air crashes	N/NV	8	3
Intern. pol. conflict	N/NV	8	3
Peace moves	N/NV	7	3
Crime and police	N/NV	7	3
Elections	N/NV	5	3
Entertainment	N/NV	3	3
Diplomatic/political	N/NV	20	2
Diplomatic/political	N/NV	14	2
Crime and police	N/NV	13	2
Religion	N/NV	12	2
Intern. pol. conflict	N/NV	11	2
Intern. pol. conflict	N/NV	10	2
Intern. pol. conflict	N/NV	7	2
Crime and police	N/NV	6	2
Sport	N/NV	4	2
Intern. pol. conflict	N/NV	9	1
Intern. pol. conflict	N/NV	9	1
Intern. pol. conflict	N/NV	7	1
Intern. pol. conflict	N/NV	7	1
Other political	N/NV	6	1
Elections	N/NV	6	1
Intern. pol. conflict	N/NV	6	1
Intern. pol. conflict	S/NV	6	1
Intern. pol. conflict	N/NV	6	1
Elections	S/NV	1	1
Crime and police	S/NV	1	1

```
N  = news items originating in the northern hemisphere
S  = news items originating in the southern hemisphere
V  = news items involving violence
NV = news items not involving violence
Detailed definitions are given in the methodological note.
```

with 14.3 percent, but only thirty paragraphs. Diplomatic and political affairs are also given some prominence with 10.7 percent of rated items, as are elections, also with 10.7 percent.

In *Le Courier de l'Ouest* most prominence is given to diplomatic and political affairs with thirty-nine paragraphs and 20.5 percent of items rated for prominence. This is followed by elections with 17.6 percent, crime with 11.8 percent and internal political conflict with only 5.9 percent.

On the whole, there is not a great deal that can be inferred from this analysis of prominence in the three newspapers, except that the Evansville *Courier* seems to have the most balanced coverage, while the *Eastern Daily Press* has the most lopsided approach to prominence with its heavy emphasis on internal political conflict. Perhaps the other remark that could be added is that the range of topics to which prominence is given is extremely varied. *Le Courier de l'Ouest* gives some degree of prominence to seventeen different subject categories, the Evansville *Courier* covers fifteen categories, while even the *Eastern Daily Press*, with its strong emphasis on internal political conflict, gives attention to ten different categories of news.

All these items were also coded for origin and violence, that is, whether they originated in a Third World or industrialized nation, classified as belonging to the northern or southern hemisphere, and whether or not they involved violence. The purpose of this was to enable comparison with the results of the above-cited study by Wilhoit and Weaver. This study, which refutes the claim that the bulk of foreign news is made up of coups and earthquakes as suggested by Mort Rosenblum,[5] concludes that foreign news coverage in small newspapers is generally very similar to coverage in the wire services that supply them with news. The study found, however, that the newspapers tend to give greater emphasis to stories of violence originating in developing nations than do the wire services.

Consequently, one of the aims of the present study is to determine whether this is true of regional newspapers in other countries. Coding for origin and violence was done not only for those newspaper stories given prominence ratings, but also for *all* foreign news items printed by the newspapers or moved by the wire services. Overall results are given in Table 8.

Origin and Violence

Generally speaking, Table 8 shows that all the newspapers and wire services analyzed report more northern hemisphere

Table 8
Types of News—Origin and Violence

Percentages

	AFP	AP	FAP	PA	EC	EDP	CO	ALL
Total north	69.4	57.9	74.0	73.3	57.9	70.5	78.6	69.9
Total south	29.1	42.6	24.8	27.1	40.5	30.1	20.8	29.8
Total violent	7 8	13.6	6.7	12.2	18.3	15.4	14.5	10.5
Total non-violent	90.7	86.9	92.1	88.2	81.1	85.2	84.9	89.2
Violent north	1.3	1.8	3.0	3.1	8.5	6.9	8.9	2.9
Violent south	6.5	11.8	3.7	9.1	9.8	8.5	5.6	7.6
Non-violent north	68.1	56.1	71.0	70.2	50.4	63.6	69.7	67.0
Non-violent south	22.6	30.8	21.1	18.0	30.7	21.6	15.2	22.2

AFP = Agence France Presse   EC = Evansville Courier
AP = Associated Press   EDP = Eastern Daily Press
FAP = French service of AP   CO = Courier de l'Ouest
PA = Press Association   ALL = All media together

Detailed definitions of violence and origin are given
in the methodological note at the end of the study.

news than southern hemisphere news. This is in keeping with the findings of major studies in this area by Sreberny-Moham-madi et al., Stevenson and Shaw and Gerbner and Marvanyi.[6] It is interesting to note, though, that the Evansville *Courier* and the wire service from which it takes its foreign news, the Associated Press, have a much more balanced coverage of north and south than do the others. Both the *Courier* and the AP devote only 57.9 percent of their coverage to the northern hemisphere, as against 70.5 percent for the *Eastern Daily Press* and 78.6 percent for *Le Courier de l'Ouest*.

With regard to violence, however, all the newspapers report more violent news than the agencies to which they subscribe. *Le Courier de l'Ouest* reports 14.5 percent as against 7.8 percent for AFP and 6.7 percent for AP's French service. The Evansville *Courier* reports 18.3 percent compared with AP's 13.6 percent.

The *Eastern Daily Press* shows 15.4 percent and the Press As-sociation 12.2 percent. These differences are slight but their con-sistency lends them significance. This tendency is in accord with the findings of the Wilhoit and Weaver study.

What is perhaps unexpected in the light of the Wilhoit and Weaver study, as well as other "coups and earthquakes" studies that appeared in the wake of the UNESCO controversy over the "free and balanced flow of information,"[7] is the relatively small amount of coverage devoted to violent news from the southern hemisphere. It is true that, with the exception of *Le Courier de l'Ouest*, all the media vehicles analyzed devote more space to violent news from the southern hemisphere than violent news from the northern hemisphere. This imbalance, although slight, is more pronounced in the wire services than the newspapers, the largest occurring in AP, with 11.8 percent devoted to violent south and 1.8 percent to violent north. All the newspapers are much more balanced in their proportions of violent north to violent south, and *Le Courier de l'Ouest* actually devotes more space to violent news from the northern hemisphere than from the southern hemisphere. This finding, in conjunction with the previous conclusion—that the newspapers devote more space to violence than do the wire services—suggests that the news-papers are more interested in violence per se than in geographic origin.

It should be stressed, however, that, with the possible excep-tion of the Evansville *Courier*, with 18.3 percent, violent news represents a relatively small proportion of overall news coverage in the newspapers. This is also reflected in the data in Tables 5, 6 and 7, which show that only very few of the news items given any prominence involve violence. In *Le Courier de l'Ouest*, only five of the thirty-four items given a prominence rating involve violence, and, incidentally, four of those five originated in a northern hemisphere country. The Evansville *Courier* shows three violent news items out of a total of twenty-eight given prominence. Of those three, two are from the southern hemi-sphere. The *Eastern Daily Press* has only one violent piece, out of a total of thirty-four, and it is from the northern hemisphere.

In summary then, the three regional newspapers studied de-vote more coverage to violence generally than do the wire services, but this coverage is not slanted toward the Third World, as is the case with the news agencies. These findings hold true for all three newspapers.

SURVEY

Twenty-three journalists working on regional newspapers in France, Britain and the United States were asked to complete a survey questionnaire indicating the qualities they sought when selecting foreign or domestic news items from a wire service, as well as some of the factors likely to affect their choice. Only journalists who regularly select foreign news were approached. They were asked to rank these qualities and influences and then to identify those features likely to make them reject a news item. Finally, they were asked to define *news*.

In some ways, the results of this survey are disappointing, partly because of uneven response. Altogether, twenty-three journalists were approached. Four out of eight British journalists responded, as did eight out of eight French journalists and five out of seven U.S. journalists. Also, some of the respondents appeared to have difficulty with the notion of ranking, even though it was carefully explained. Despite these weaknesses, quite a lot of information can be gained from the questionnaire, a copy of which is to be found in the methodological note at the end of the study.

Because of inconsistencies in rankings, the results of the survey given in Table 9 show only how many journalists in each country believe that the factors indicated affect their selection of news items. Although this does not give an actual ranking, it does give an idea of which factors are considered to be the most important and it does allow some form of rough comparison between the journalists of each country.

Perhaps the most obvious conclusion that can be drawn from Table 9 is that the criteria used for the selection of foreign news are very similar to those used for the selection of domestic news. Furthermore, with a few minor exceptions, British, French and U.S. journalists all seem to give importance to the same criteria They all appear to believe that accuracy, topicality, human interest and local impact are the most important criteria. Length

Table 9

Journalists' Opinion of Qualities Affecting News Selection

Number of journalists who believe that the factors
indicated affect their selection of news items.

I - Qualities affecting the selection of domestic news

	Britain (total 4)	France (total 8)	U.S. (total 5)
Accuracy	3	8	5
How topical	4	8	5
Local impact	4	7	5
Length	1	3	2
Human interest	4	8	4
Byline	0	1	3
Geographic origin	3	4	3

II - Qualities affecting the selection of foreign news

	Britain (total 4)	France (total 8)	U.S. (total 5)
Accuracy	4	7	5
How topical	4	8	5
Local impact	2	6	5
Length	0	1	2
Human interest	4	8	5
Byline	0	0	3
Geographic origin	3	7	4

III - Factors guiding the selection of news

	Britain (total 4)	France (total 8)	U.S. (total 5)
Editorial policy	4	6	3
Professional training	3	6	4
Immediate supervisor	2	2	4
Fellow journalists	0	1	4
Personal convictions	3	7	4
Readers´ interest	4	8	5

and byline, on the other hand, do not seem to be very influential, although U.S. journalists are seen to be more affected by byline than their British or French counterparts. Geographic origin is accorded some importance for foreign news.

Among the external factors affecting selection, readers' interest is viewed by all respondents as the most important, followed by personal convictions and professional training. Editorial policy is also accorded some importance by all the respondents. The influence of peers is seen as negligible by the British and French journalists, but U.S. journalists view it as fairly important. On the whole, U.S. journalists seem to feel that they are influenced by more of these factors than do journalists in Britain and France, which may be an indication of less individualism and a greater sense of professionalism among U.S. journalists.

Probably what is most interesting about the findings of this survey, given the different journalistic images and traditions referred to in previous chapters, is that the responses are so similar. The journalists were asked to give a definition of *news*. The fact that the definitions given are all so different could be taken, simplistically, as a sign of dissimilarity, but it is probably more indicative of an underlying trait common to all journalists, that of individualism.

Although not much can be inferred from them, these definitions of news are reproduced below for their instrinsic interest. The actual question asked of the journalists was: "Finally, how would you define *news*?"

Britain

"An event that catches you off guard. The unusual" (*Eastern Daily Press*).

"What other people are doing that either affects or reflects on the way we live" (*Eastern Daily Press*).

"News is a story which will, on reading, appeal to a considerable number of people and form talking points amongst them. Preferably concerning a subject about which they would have been uninformed, or ill-informed, if it had not been printed in our newspaper" (The *Yorkshire Post*).

"With great difficulty; probably something which captures the public imagination or emotions; or something which affects people's everyday lives" (The *Yorkshire Post*).

France

"A photograph of the present. Like all photographs, it shows only certain aspects of reality" (*Le Courier de l'Ouest*).

"A meal which must be eaten hot" (*Le Courier de l'Ouest*).

"The important events of the day" (*Le Courier de l'Ouest*).

"That which will happen tomorrow" (*Le Télégramme de Brest*)

"That which is accurate, short, impartial, factual"(*Le Maine Libre*).

"That which offers an immediate interest for the greatest number and which, at the same time, is likely to have long-term consequences" (*Presse-Océan*).

"That which goes from the general interest to the particular interest" (*Ouest-France*).

"Information that is new for the reader" (*Ouest-France*).

United States

"An event that is important, informative or interesting" (Evansville *Courier*).

"Any event that is relevant to or of interest to the reader" (Evansville *Courier*).

"What is different today from yesterday. Change. Also, a gut feeling about what topics are on people's minds" (*Courier-Journal*).

NOTE. Only three of the U.S. journalists chose to answer this question.

OBSERVATION

During the course of the above discussion, it has been suggested that some of the divergences noted in the content analysis are probably the result of different criteria used by journalists when selecting foreign news items from a wire service. Those identified include general editorial policy, the length and style of wire service dispatches, and the personal preferences and idiosyncracies of individual journalists.

As has been pointed out already, the divergences of content between newspapers and their wire services, or among the different newspapers, are not only few but generally minor and, therefore, are not very useful in determining other criteria. However, the wealth of information produced by lengthy periods of observation and interviews with journalists makes it possible to fill in the gaps and develop a complete list of influences affecting the selection of foreign news. Some of these are environmental or structural, some are professional and personal, and some are intrinsic to news items themselves.

In Chapter 1, it was pointed out that there is now a considerable body of research on why journalists make the editorial choices they do. It might be useful at this point to recall some of the highlights of this literature. In his landmark gatekeeper study in 1950, David Manning White reluctantly concluded that the selection of news was a highly subjective process strongly influenced by the gatekeeper's own experiences, attitudes and expectations rather than by organizational constraints.[8] A few years later, Warren Breed suggested that individual journalists were affected by socializing forces in the newsroom.[9] The British sociologist Jeremy Tunstall has shown the influence of peers or "competitor-colleagues" among specialist correspondents.[10]

More recently, Cohen and Young, Golding and Elliott, Tuchman, and Fishman have studied the "manufacture" of news, which has thus become viewed as a construction rather than a reflection of social reality.[11] Philip Schlesinger has described the "mediation of control" as it affects editorial policies,[12] while media critic Ben Bagdikian believes that news is manipulated by a "private ministry of information" whose members are the leaders of business and industry linked together through "interlocking directorates."[13] Altschull has argued that the media have become agents of those forces that wield power in the economic, political, social and cultural environment.[14] With regard to influences on individual journalists, Herbert Gans has defined eight clusters of "enduring values" that affect the production of news.[15]

The above examples of research represent trends in the study of communicators, either as individuals or as actors within an organization or a society. However, these research trends tend to remain separated from each other and little, if anything, has been done to explore how different influences affect each other. In *Individuals in Mass Media Organizations*, Charles Whitney makes a plea for researchers to identify different levels of analysis when studying communicators.[16] Paul Hirsch, too, has argued in favor of linking occupational, organizational and institutional models of mass media research.[17] On a less strictly theoretical level, Gertrude Joch Robinson has attempted to separate environmental factors from internal organization factors.

Environmental factors, like ownership patterns, circulation size, availability of technical facilities for international news purchase and exchange, the deployment of the foreign correspondent corps and a country's diplomatic history and relations all limit the availability of foreign news. Organizational selection practices and the professional values of the staff on the other hand determine allotment of news space to foreign affairs, particular geographical selection and idiosyncratic subject matter focuses.[18]

In an earlier study, Robinson and Sparkes categorized factors affecting international news flow into four groups: technico-economic, political-historical, editorial weighting, and market-place or audience factors.[19]

Such contributions are valuable but, while they bring some order to the wide array of factors that affect news selection, they fail to explain how the factors affect each other. The rest of this chapter suggests a simple new taxonomy that makes it possible to understand the interactions that occur among the many influences identified during observation and interviews.

Before doing so, two preliminary remarks should be made. The first is that most of the journalists interviewed have very little idea of why they select the news they do. This is not surprising given the complexities of the news selection process. Typically, they have never taken the time to think about it, and if they do, they often refer to some kind of "news sense" or "nose" or "instinct," which may not be far from the truth because the news selection process is governed more by a body of "tacit knowledge" than by a set of precise rules and procedures.

The second remark is that a great deal of confusion exists over terminology. Researchers give different meanings to such terms as values, criteria, influences, determinants or factors. Sometimes they are used interchangeably; sometimes they are given very precise shades of meaning. Sometimes researchers agree on what they mean; more frequently they do not. Furthermore, terms used to describe categories, such as "organizational" or "professional" are often ambiguous or have unclear boundaries.

What is proposed here is a taxonomy of factors grouped into three categories: managerial influences, professional-personal values, and intrinsic news characteristics. First, these different influences, values and characteristics will be identified, using data collected during interviews and observation. Then it will be shown how this taxonomy can be used to better explain and understand interactions among the various factors involved.

MANAGERIAL INFLUENCES ON CONTENT

This group includes such management-decided factors as technology, deadlines and newshole. They are external to editorial decisions, but have a definite effect upon them. The term "managerial" is used instead of "organizational" because the factors included in this group are all manifestly the result of management decisions, whereas "organizational" is often used to describe factors such as newsroom hierarchy or socialization, which belong more properly to the professional-personal group.

Space and Newshole

These are twin aspects of a management-generated constraint that affects both foreign and domestic news. The number of pages of an edition is fixed in advance according to newshole requirements and advertising projections. On the one hand, there is usually not enough space, with the result that advertising and editorial departments have to fight for what is available. On the other hand, newshole has increased while newsroom staffs have remained stable or actually decreased, thus putting more pressure on individual journalists.

In this constant struggle to find or fill space, foreign news is usually the first to go. In all three newspapers observed, foreign news is considered to be less important than domestic news, either national or local. It is there because it is felt that a newspaper ought to have *some* foreign news, but in the absence of genuinely important international events, it usually takes the form of a column of world briefs thrown together early in the evening. However, at times, when an unexpectedly large newshole becomes available because of an unusually large edition or a drop in advertising, the copy desk can be observed scrambling for foreign news items to use as fillers.

Technology

Electronic news processing systems, introduced by profit-conscious management, now enable overworked newsroom staff to select and edit foreign news items with a minimum of trouble. Most of the journalists observed liked to get their column of world briefs locked up as early as possible, with the result that news that moved in the early part of the evening tended to be used. Although, in theory, electronic news processing makes it easier to edit, very little editing or rewriting was observed. In fact, paradoxically, there appeared to be more rewriting at *Le Courier de l'Ouest*, which had not yet gone fully electronic, than at either the *Eastern Daily Press* or the Evansville *Courier*.

Agency Selection

As was seen from the results of the content analysis, foreign news coverage in the newspapers studied closely matches that of the wire services to which they subscribe. The fact that the international news agencies appear to be becoming more and more similar may account for the homogeneity of coverage that emerges from the content analysis, as does the fact that there seems to be little editing or rewriting of agency copy, apart from simple trimming. However, insofar as certain divergences do continue to exist, the choice of a particular agency, or agencies, may have an effect upon foreign news coverage.

Mandatory Copy

Ownership by or affiliation to a certain group may encourage the use of syndicated copy. For example, at the Evansville *Courier*, which is owned by Scripps-Howard, the copy desk was strongly encouraged to use Scripps-Howard material rather than

AP copy whenever possible. At *Le Courier de l'Ouest*, too, on more than one occasion management sent down a syndicated piece with orders to print it.

Foreign Correspondents

It is rare for regional newspapers to have full-time foreign correspondents, but, from time to time, staff reporters get to travel overseas and, on these occasions, any copy they file is highly likely to be printed. Angers, where *Le Courier de l'Ouest* is published, is also home to an army regiment that periodically sends units overseas, often accompanied by a *Courier* reporter. The newspaper has published several articles not only about the activities of the regiment but also about the countries in which they have been posted. *Ouest-France*, published in Rennes, has its own correspondents in several foreign countries and, as a result, tends to have more coverage of those countries than other parts of the world. The Evansville *Courier* has taken advantage of Indiana trade missions to print a special issue on the Far East. Not only does the existence of correspondents and foreign travel produce specific coverage of overseas events, it also promotes an ongoing interest in areas covered, and, as a result, future stories about those areas tend to receive preferential treatment.

Foreign Editor

The existence of a foreign editor, although rare in regional newspapers, is also likely to affect overall foreign news content. Typically, the foreign editor supervises the work of foreign correspondents and may have little to do with the routine selection of foreign news from agency copy. More important, however, the presence of a foreign editor at editorial conferences, where space is allocated and fought for, usually makes for increased foreign news coverage. This is certainly the case at *Ouest-France*, whose foreign editor favors lengthy, well-written analytical foreign news stories rather than world briefs taken straight from the wire. It is to be noted that when the foreign editor is absent there is less foreign news in the newspaper. The situation is somewhat similar at the *Yorkshire Post*, which has a specialized foreign subeditor as well as three staff editorialists (leader writers), all of whom take a strong interest in foreign news. Foreign news appears on the important op-ed page and usually includes at least one foreign editorial. At smaller newspapers, without specialized foreign editorial staff, foreign news is given less priority.

General Editorial Policy

It is not often that regional newspapers have firm policies on foreign news, mainly because foreign news is generally considered to be of little importance. However, it is not unknown for individual publishers to develop a strong personal interest in a given country or region. The Bingham family, which used to own the *Courier-Journal* in Louisville before it was sold to Gannett, was said to be extraordinarily fond of Britain and France. Although journalists who were with the newspaper at that time can recall no specific directives from the publisher, news items and articles about those two countries appeared with great frequency. However, this kind of influence is rapidly disappearing as ownership passes from private to corporate hands, and as personal interests are subordinated to group objectives.

Deadlines

Electronic news management allows later deadlines because it makes it possible to change or replace copy at the last minute. This tends to favor late local news, particularly in competitive situations, but foreign news suffers because it is usually finalized much earlier than local news. At both the *Eastern Daily Press* and the Evansville *Courier*, those pages containing world briefs are locked up well in advance of other pages, the general feeling being that foreign news can keep longer than national or local news. At *Le Courier de l'Ouest*, which at the time of observation had direct input only in the branch offices, the foreign news page was described as a "cold page," while local pages were kept open until the very last minute, particularly in those editions having to compete with other newspapers.

Sunday Editions

Only one of the three newspapers observed, the Evansville *Courier*, has a Sunday edition. Although, a priori, the existence of a Sunday edition may not appear to have any relevance to foreign news coverage, conversations with *Courier* staffers revealed that, when space was tight, foreign news items were held back for Sunday. Sunday was regarded as a slow news day, so saving foreign news stories until then was seen to fulfill the double function of providing fillers for the Sunday edition while easing pressure on space during the week. This might possibly explain why the number of foreign news items in the Evansville *Courier* is 34 percent lower than that of *Le Courier de l'Ouest* and 38 percent lower than that of the *Eastern Daily Press*, but such an explanation cannot be advanced with any certainty.

Staffing

Staffing is closely related to all the other factors already reviewed, and, like them, is governed by management decisions. Obviously, for reasons of profitability, it is desirable to reduce staffing to a minimum, and this can be achieved with electronic news systems and routine sources. However, the smaller the staff and the greater the degree of routinization, the more homogenized news coverage becomes, and this is particularly true for foreign news. Observation suggests that foreign news coverage in regional newspapers has been largely reduced to "pick and print," a close relative of the "rip and read" technique practiced in most small radio stations.

Time

Time is a factor that is closely related to many of the other influences described above and, because it is largely a function of staffing, editorial policy, deadlines and technology, it is one that is determined by management. All the journalists observed and interviewed, without exception, felt that they did not have enough time to do their jobs properly. Most of them stated that if they had more time they would do more rewriting, particularly of foreign news items, instead of just editing for length.

Image of the Organization

The self-image of a newspaper, which is the result of past and present management attitudes and decisions, can have a profound effect upon foreign news coverage. This affirmation is strongly supported by evidence gathered during observation. The *Yorkshire Post* published in Leeds is read by "expatriate" Yorkshire people in other parts of the country and has a full-fledged London office, but it is essentially a local, metropolitan newspaper. However, it is considered, and considers itself, as an "influential" newspaper whose opinion counts. It employs three full-time foreign news specialists and, as a result, its foreign news coverage tends to be extensive. The *Eastern Daily Press*, which has virtually the same circulation, and which may be the most successful provincial morning newspaper in the country at the moment, does not have the same big newspaper image and employs no foreign news specialists. Its foreign coverage, while adequate, is nowhere near as extensive or as in-depth as that of the *Yorkshire Post*.

Similarly, the *Courier-Journal* of Louisville, which has long thought of itself as the *New York Times* of the Midwest, believes it has a mission to provide extensive foreign news coverage, while the Indianapolis *Star*, which has roughly the same circulation and which views itself as a large metropolitan newspaper, does not give the same priority to foreign news. In France too, *Ouest-France*, which is basically a regional newspaper, even if it has a very large circulation, considers itself to be "important" and has a very sophisticated and particularly competent foreign news staff, including foreign correspondents. Its foreign news coverage is exemplary. *Le Courier de l'Ouest*, on the other hand, which is a very successful newspaper, claims no "mission" beyond its circulation area and gives relatively low priority to foreign news.

PROFESSIONAL-PERSONAL VALUES OF JOURNALISTS

The factors included in this group are often thought of as those that have the most influence in determining news content. The selection of news items is of course affected by professional training, personal convictions and newsroom socialization, but it will be argued later that these factors are themselves affected by the structural influences described above.

Training

As was seen in a previous chapter, criteria used in the selection of news are fostered and strengthened by professional training. These criteria tend to be the same within a given culture, but may vary from one culture to another. Not all journalists receive training. All the U.S. journalists interviewed had received some degree of professional training, most of them at college level. Among the British journalists, many had taken training courses on release from jobs, but few had been to a university. In France, the majority of journalists interviewed had *not* received any specialized professional training but many had a university diploma of some sort. While professional training should make for homogeneous news selection, different levels of training, combined with other forms of education, are more likely to produce variation.

Personal Convictions

D.M. White's previously cited study[20] suggests that personal convictions are important in guiding editorial decisions. This was certainly found to be true in the newspapers observed. At the *Eastern Daily Press*, one of the journalists responsible for foreign news selection rejected a story about missiles because, he said, "Missiles bore me!" But he put in a story about the environment because "They [the readers] ought to be interested." At *Le Courier de l'Ouest* one of the foreign news journalists rejected a story about an American criminal condemned to death for the rape and murder of a thirteen year old, but suggested that her colleague, who did the foreign news when she was off, would probably have used it. At the Evansville *Courier*, personal convictions seemed to be less influential but, nonetheless, copy desk journalists stated that stories about Chad were often used because, for some idiosyncratic reason, they appealed to the assistant managing editor for news.

Personal Capacities

Individual work habits, attitudes and capacities may also affect news selection. The most striking example was at the *Eastern Daily Press* where the two journalists responsible for foreign news demonstrated very different approaches. One tended to select too many stories during the first sort and then had to eliminate some. The other appeared to be far more critical and sometimes had trouble filling the space allotted to foreign news. At *Le Courier de l'Ouest*, one of the journalists liked to arrive early and get the world briefs out of the way as soon as possible. The other preferred to leave them until later so as not to miss any late news. At the Evansville *Courier*, news selection procedures appeared to be less idiosyncratic.

Newsroom Forces

In a previously cited study, Warren Breed explored the social forces at work in the newsroom.[21] Socialization can take many forms that may not be immediately obvious, but, even with this in mind, observation revealed significant differences between the newsrooms studied. The most noticeable was in the degree of interaction among journalists. At the Evansville *Courier*, there was a constant exchange of ideas and suggestions around the copy desk so that news—even foreign news—seemed to emerge as the result of a consensus. At the *Eastern Daily Press*, on the other hand, the journalist reponsible for foreign (and national) news worked very much on his own. Although located at the top desk at one end of a very busy newsroom, the foreign news editor hardly raised his eyes from his screen all night and spoke only rarely to others. Decisions concerning foreign news were taken therefore in isolation, without any consensus or brokering. At *Le Courier de l'Ouest*, the situation was different again. Here, the journalist responsible for foreign news selection sorted agency dispatches by hand without any reference to the other journalists. The only interchange that took place concerned the way in which a particular story should be edited.

It is at this level that hierarchical forces come into play. In all three newspapers it was observed that the slotman or chief sub-editor or page-one editor enjoyed unquestioned authority. Even in those cases where news was the result of a consensus, the editor's word was final. Such senior people share many years of experience—and socialization. It is through their authority that the socialized habits of individual newsrooms, including foreign news selection, are passed on to younger journalists.

Readership Perceptions

The survey questionnaires analyzed earlier in this chapter showed that all respondents considered readers' interest to be a very important factor in determining news content. During interviews and observation, frequent mention was made of readers' preferences, but journalists' ideas of what readers actually wanted seemed to be very subjective in all cases. The Evansville *Courier* has not done any recent audience research. Both the *Eastern Daily Press* and *Le Courier de l'Ouest* conduct regular professional surveys, and management uses the results to shape editorial policy. However, individual journalists do not seem to be familiar with the findings of such research.

Journalistic Image

The image that journalists have of themselves also affects the way in which they select news. "Watchdogs" may favor news items that challenge the workings of government and public institutions, even in foreign countries. "Reporters" may attempt to provide an evenhanded mix of news. "Interpreters" may prefer stories that explain a certain situation or provide context to an overall view of the world.

INTRINSIC NEWS CHARACTERISTICS OF NEWS ITEMS

All news stories have instrinsic characteristics that make them more or less attractive to different journalists in different media vehicles. Some of these characteristics are common to all news stories; others are more specific to foreign news.

Newsworthiness

Although difficult to define with any precision, newsworthiness is generally associated with such notions as the unusual or unexpected, timeliness, accuracy, proximity and audience impact. Journalists are trained to recognize these features, and if a story does not possess at least some of them, it is unlikely to be used. For foreign news, timeliness may be less important, unless it is a major story, because most of the journalists interviewed felt that foreign news keeps better than national or local news. The news editor at the Evanvsille *Courier* cited a survey that had been presented at a meeting of news editors indicating that readers do not really mind when they get news provided they are brought up to date. Proximity is a related concept in that the further away the news the less urgent it is. However, with regard to foreign news, proximity may have more to do with cultural or ethnic affinity than with actual distance.

External Factors

The selection of foreign news in any country is affected by the special ties that exist between that country and its allies, trading partners or former colonial possessions. Journalists interviewed at British newspapers admitted that they gave preferential treatment to news from members of the Commonwealth, such as Australia and South Africa, or to former colonial possessions, such as India or Kenya, or again to strategic bases, such as Cyprus or Gibraltar. Interest in the United States is also high, partly because of the "special relationship" that exists between the two countries, but also because of America's status as a world power.

In the same way, French journalists seek out news from the Maghreb, certain West African countries, Indochina, and such overseas territories as New Caledonia and the French West Indies. Like other Western journalists, they also have a great interest in the world's major powers. In fact, there is a general rule that the larger and the more influential a country, the more newsworthy it becomes, no doubt because its actions are more likely to affect other countries.

The United States has no former colonies, but it has a particular interest in certain countries for strategic, ideological, commercial and ethnic reasons, and this interest is certainly reflected in the selection of foreign news. Strategic and ideological reasons tend to become confused in such geographic areas as Central America and Southeast Asia where defense is aimed more against the threat of communism than territorial invasion. But news coverage remains high in the wire services and, therefore, in newspaper news content. Commercial concerns lead to emphasis on such countries as Japan and Taiwan, while Latin America has long been considered a U.S. preserve.

Beyond these factors, ethnic considerations are much more influential in foreign news in the United States than in the other countries studied. Being a nation of immigrants, there is a high level of interest in "the old country," which means largely Britain, Germany, Italy and Ireland, but also Poland, Greece, Lithuania and Sweden, as well as many other homelands. Journalists interviewed stated that they did not go out of their way to find news about any particular country, except for Europe in general and Britain in particular, but this probably depends a great deal on the area in which a newspaper is published. There is likely to be more of an interest in Poland in Chicago than in Atlanta.

One other influence that is particularly marked in the United States is the presence of a powerful and articulate Jewish community. This creates a strong interest in Israel, not only on strategic grounds but also as a privileged partner. It also gives emphasis to Jewish affairs around the world, and, in particular, the plight of Jews in Soviet bloc countries. Once again, this influence may be stronger in certain cities than others.

Format

Given the time and space constraints on foreign news, preference is frequently given to stories that have the right length and style, and are easy to cut. Observation confirmed that, when filling a world briefs column, journalists tended to select news items that could be slotted right in with a minimum of trouble, provided, of course, that they met the criteria of newsworthiness and interest described above.

One particularly important feature is the inverted pyramid style, which enables an editor to trim a story from the bottom. It was noticeable at *Le Courier de l'Ouest*, which takes both AFP and the French service of AP, that journalists often preferred to take foreign briefs from the AP wire while more elaborate stories were taken from AFP. The explanation for this is that the French service of the AP tends to use the inverted pyramid style much more than AFP which, although it has made changes in the last few years, still clings to a more discursive style. In so far as wire services set foreign news agendas to a large degree, the fact that a wire service is selected for reasons of format could have an important effect upon the foreign news content of a newspaper.

Availability of News Story

Finally, foreign news coverage will depend upon the availability of foreign news in the wire service or services taken by a newspaper. It could be objected that this is an external structural factor, but the journalist faced with the problem of selecting news must regard the existence or nonexistence of a news story as one of its most essential intrinsic characteristics. Robinson and Sparkes have pointed to the importance of the deployment of correspondents as a determinant of foreign news,[22] and, in this respect, it could be said that news is what is covered, where it is covered. The question of the agenda-setting function of the wire services, particularly with regard to foreign news, is one that deserves discussion, and it is one about which more will be said later. Meanwhile, for the the journalist on the desk, news is what is available. Two striking examples of this were furnished by observation at the Evansville *Courier* and *Le Courier de l'Ouest*.

One of the observation days spent at the Evansville *Courier* was Memorial Day, which, domestically, turned out to be a very slow news day, as holidays often are. The biggest story of the day was the summit meeting taking place in Moscow. Even though the newspaper was only twenty-two pages that day, the copy desk found itself scrambling for news. In the absence of much national news, far more foreign news was used than normal. At *Le Courier de l'Ouest* no newspaper was published on Ascension Day, which meant that, on that day, as preparations were made for the following morning's newspaper, there were two days of news to process. In this case, with more than enough domestic news available, less foreign news was used.

In the same way, although this was not observed, it could be expected that public holidays in foreign countries would lead to a lack of available news from those countries.

Public Image of Journalism

The concept of image is an important one that has been discussed at some length in Chapter 2. It has been shown that the self-image of an organization can have a profound effect upon foreign news coverage and that the image of the individual journalist can also have a marked influence on the way in which news is processed. How journalists think of themselves will depend on the society in which they live, the image of the press in general and the image of the organization in which they work. The public's image of journalism, and the way in which that image is perceived, can help to shape the foreign news agenda from which individual journalists have to make a selection.

This discussion of image is particularly useful because it shows how the various factors listed in Table 10 interact with one another, sometimes in a circular fashion. In previous research, there has been a tendency to view the influences affecting news content as independent factors acting directly upon the news selection process. Observation carried out in the newsrooms of three different newspapers in three different countries suggests that these factors are interdependent, and that many of them affect the news selection process only indirectly.

The factors listed in Table 10 are grouped under four headings: managerial influences, professional/personal values, intrinsic news characteristics and "exogenous" factors. It is argued that the actual selection process is guided by professional and personal values, as researchers such as White, Breed, Gans, Tuch-

Table 10
A Taxonomy of Factors Affecting Foreign News Content

Exogenous factors	Managerial influences	Professional/ personal values	Intrinsic news characteristics
COMPETITION	space/newshole	training	newsworthiness · timeliness · proximity · impact · unexpected etc.
	technology	personal convictions	
	agency selection	personal capacities	external factors · historical · political · economic · ethnic
PROFIT ========>	mandatory copy	newsroom forces · hierarchy · socialization · consensus	
	foreign correspondents		
	foreign editor	readership perceptions	format · length · style · easy to cut
	editorial policy	journalistic image	
	deadlines		availability of news story
OWNERSHIP	Sunday edition		public image of journalism
	staffing/time		
	image of the organization		

man, Tunstall and many others have found, but that these values are *constrained* by a number of managerial influences, and *defined* by the intrinsic characteristics of the news items they are selecting. Furthermore, intrinsic news characteristics may also be a factor in those decisions that determine managerial influences. Finally, the entire news selection process is shaped by the twin "exogenous" factors of competition and ownership—and their joint alter ego profit—which affect not only individual newspapers but also the whole environment of the Western media.

It is easy to see how these groups of factors interact with one another. For example, mandatory copy, imposed by group ownership, may override professional training and personal convictions and negate the newsworthiness of a particular story. However, at the same time, management's decision to impose mandatory copy may well be tempered by considerations of newsworthiness. There is a definite dynamic interchange in this process.

In the same way, a decision to reduce staffing, because of competition, may encourage a beleaguered journalist to select a story because of its format rather than its newsworthiness. Or, readership perceptions, shaped by editorial policy and the newspaper's image, may prompt a journalist to select a news item for political or ethnic reasons rather than for other reasons. Or again, a strongly professional journalistic image, particularly if combined with an organizational image of hard news, may result in the selection of items because of their qualities of newsworthiness rather than their format or historico-political features. Or, finally, the existence of rigid editorial policies may run counter to personal convictions, training and newsroom consensus and lead to the selection of certain types of ethnic or political items. It can be seen that many different combinations of factors are possible.

Professional and personal values, which are closest to the point of decision in the news selection process, are those that are most likely to produce differences in news content. Previous chapters have argued that these values *are* somewhat different in the three countries studied, but, as content analysis has shown, there is little if any divergence in the news content of their newspapers, at least in terms of subject matter categories.

What appears to be happening is that these individualistic values are "flattened" by managerial influences that are emerging in response to the external factors of group ownership and competition. The result is greater homogeneity of news content. Given the profit-oriented structure of the media, this result is perhaps inevitable, but there may be other alternatives, as the final chapter of this book suggests.

NOTES

1. Interview with Yves Gacon, editor in chief, France, Agence France Presse.

2. Interview with Pierre Legros, director of the French service of Associated Press.

3. Wilhoit and Weaver, "Foreign News Coverage in Two U.S. News Services: An Update," pp. 132–148.

4. See in particular Richard W. Budd, "Attention Score: A Device for Measuring News Play," *Journalism Quarterly* 41:2 (Spring 1964), pp. 259–262. A further discussion of the relevant parts of this article is given in the methodology note at the end of the study.

5. Rosenblum, *Coups and Earthquakes*.

6. In particular, see Sreberny-Mohammadi et al., "Foreign News in the Media"; Stevenson and Shaw, *Foreign News and the New World Information Order*; Gerbner and Marvanyi, "The Many Worlds of the World's Press."

7. Among many others, Jim Richstad and Michael A. Anderson (eds.), *Crisis in International News: Policies and Prospects* (New York: Columbia University Press, 1981); Mustapha Masmoudi, "The New World Information Order," *Journal of Communication* 29:2 (Spring 1979), pp. 172–185; Smith, *The Geopolitics of Information: How Western Culture Dominates the World*.

8. White, "The Gate-Keeper."

9. Breed, "Social Control in the Newsroom."

10. Tunstall, *Journalists at Work*.

11. Stanley Cohen and Jock Young (eds.), *The Manufacture of News* (London: Constable, 1973); Peter Golding and Philip Elliott, *Making the News* (London: Longman, 1979); Gaye Tuchman, *Making News: A Study in the Construction of Reality* (New York: Free Press, 1978); Mark Fishman, *Manufacturing the News* (Austin: University of Texas Press, 1980).

12. Philip Schlesinger, *Putting Reality Together* (London: Constable, 1978).

13. Bagdikian, *The Media Monopoly*.

14. Altschull, *Agents of Power*.

15. Gans, *Deciding What's News*.

16. D. Charles Whitney, "Mass Communicator Studies: Similarity, Difference and Level of Analysis," in James S. Ettema and D. Charles Whitney (eds.), *Individuals in Mass Media Organizations: Creativity and Constraint* (Beverly Hills, Calif.: Sage, 1982).

17. Paul M. Hirsch, "Occupational, Organizational, and Institutional Models in Mass Media Resarch: Toward an Integrated Framework," in Paul M. Hirsch, Peter V. Miller and F. Gerald Kline (eds.), *Strategies for Communication Research* (Beverly Hills, Calif.: Sage, 1977).

18. Gertrude Joch Robinson, "Foreign News Values in the Quebec, English Canadian and U.S. Press: A Comparison Study," *Canadian Journal of Communication* 9:3 (1983), pp. 1–32.

19. Gertrude Joch Robinson and Vernone M. Sparkes, "International News in the Canadian and American Press: A Comparative News Flow Study," *Gazette* 22:4 (1976), pp. 203–218.

20. White, "The Gate-Keeper."

21. Breed, "Social Control in the Newsroom."

22. Robinson and Sparkes, "International News," p. 207.

7

CONCLUSIONS

Previous chapters have shown that, despite divergences in the journalistic images and traditions of Britain, France and the United States, foreign news coverage in the regional newspapers of those countries is remarkably similar, at least in subject matter. It is still not clear, though, why there is such a disparity between journalistic images and procedures. This chapter argues that professional procedures are changing more rapidly than journalistic images because of a number of new influences that have emerged from changing patterns of ownership and a climate of increased competition.

FACTORS AFFECTING UNIFORMITY

Although they remain firmly entrenched in popular imagination, journalistic images in all three countries are slowly changing as journalism comes under closer scrutiny from both the public and the media themselves. But clear differences still remain. The findings reported in the last chapter, particularly those generated by observation, suggest that personal convictions tend to be a more important factor in news selection in Britain and France than in the United States, implying perhaps that British and French journalists are more independent, or less disciplined, than their American counterparts. However, there is also evidence to suggest that such differences are disappearing as a result of growing professionalization.

Changes in journalistic practices have been much more rapid. Because of increasing competition, profit-conscious group managers in all three countries have introduced new constraints and procedures that have tended to standardize news selection processes. Other related influences have also been instrumental in producing more homogeneous news coverage. It is possible to identify three general factors that are bringing uniformity to foreign news coverage. They are: management, professionalization and the agenda-setting role of the news agencies, which correspond to the three sets of factors defined in the taxonomy developed in Chapter 6, that is, managerial influences, professional/personal values, and instrinsic news characteristics.

Management

The various managerial influences listed in Chapter 6 are all the result of decisions taken to increase profitability or cope with competition, not only from newspapers but also from other media both "old" and "new." Most of these influences, such as deadlines, space, newshole and staffing, place heavy constraints on those journalists responsible for news selection. As a result, journalists tend to take the least line of resistance and select those news items that are the easiest to find and edit.

Other influences, such as agency selection, the use of mandatory copy or the existence of foreign correspondents, determine the amount and type of information available. Journalists select items that are the easiest to use from the only sources of news available to them, which, to a large extent, are dictated by management. As was argued in Chapter 6, the availability of foreign news *within* those sources is not controlled by management and is, therefore, a factor that is more closely related to the intrinsic news characteristics of a news item.

Electronic news management systems make it even more convenient to select news from electronic sources. While, in theory, electronic news systems are supposed to make it easier for journalists to merge, rewrite or otherwise edit stories, observation carried out for this study suggests that, in fact, less rewriting is done in newspapers equipped with VDTs than in those that have yet to adopt electronic news processing. This may seem paradoxical, but there is an explanation. According to many journalists interviewed, the introduction of electronic news processing has given them new tasks to perform, such as checking words and keying in complicated layout instructions, work that used to be done by linotype and composing staff. As a result, they have less time to spend on purely journalistic duties.

Professionalization

Increasing professionalization also makes for greater uniformity of coverage because it tends to iron out the personal convictions and other idiosyncrasies that result in diversity and individualism. In France, an increasing number of journalists are being exposed to some form of professional training, while in Britain increasing numbers of university graduates are entering the profession. The end result is that the profiles of journalists in France, Britain and the United States are becoming more similar.

Not only are journalists becoming more alike in their educational and social backgrounds, but they are also more inclined to espouse the same journalistic principles. For example, partly because of more widespread professional training, but also because of more exposure to "Anglo-Saxon" principles of journalism, French journalists are now more likely to write and to select inverted-pyramid style stories than they were only one or two decades ago.

The Agenda-Setting Role of the News Agencies

This and other studies have found that foreign news coverage in regional newspapers closely mirrors that of the wire services from which they take their news. With a few minor exceptions, the types and proportions of news reported are almost identical. Consequently, insofar as the foreign news reported in a newspaper is taken almost exclusively from the wire service to which it subscribes, it can be seen that the wire service plays a very major role in determining that newspaper's foreign news agenda.

Furthermore, content analysis done for this study, and reported in the previous chapter, shows that foreign news coverage in the four news agencies, Associated Press, Agence France Presse, Press Association and the French service of Associated Press, is also remarkably uniform. This offers another explanation of why the foreign news reported in the regional newspapers of three different countries is so similar. It also begs the question of who or what sets the news agenda for the wire services, but that is a question that goes far beyond the scope of this present study.

It is argued, therefore, that the subject matter uniformity of foreign news coverage in regional papers in France, Britain and the United States is the result of a combination of interrelated factors. Of these, the most important appear to be the managerial influences introduced by a new breed of commercial managers hired and trained by chain ownership to maximize profit. Taken together, these managerial influences are reshaping the criteria of news selection as well as professional values. Electronic news processing is de-emphasizing certain traditional journalistic skills, but, at the same time, it is requiring the acquisition of new skills. Meanwhile, increasing professionalization is also contributing to the standardization of news selection processes. Finally, homogeneous foreign news coverage in the wire services seems inevitably to produce homogeneous foreign news coverage in regional newspapers.

It could be argued, too, that these influences are also producing a growing Americanization of regional newspapers in France and Britain, and, possibly, by extension, of other media in other countries. Commercial management and group ownership are by no means exclusively American phenomena, but they emerged in the United States earlier than in France and Britain, where ideological and political motivations have been more powerful, or at least more overt. Today, newspaper management principles and techniques in all three countries seem to be closer than ever before, and the influences they are producing are having the same effects on professional values and news selection.

The growing professionalization noted earlier is also producing journalistic styles and images that are closer to the American model. The depoliticization of news content in British and French regional newspapers, prompted by both professional and commercial reasons, seems to be pointing the way toward an American style of journalism that separates commentary from factual reporting, and this may be one of the most important changes taking place at the present time.

Finally, the domination of the American wire services, especially that of the Associated Press, seems to be stronger than ever. In Britain, the domestic news agency, the Press Association, is a blend of not only the Reuters service but also the AP world wire. In France, the AP has its own French language service taken by a growing number of newspapers. At the same time, the French national news service, Agence France Presse, while remaining the official agency of record, has responded to growing international competition by moving steadily closer to American reporting styles. For all these reasons, the style and content of the news services studied appear to be becoming more American, and this is reflected in the foreign news content of regional newspapers.

FURTHER RESEARCH

Like many studies, this book has perhaps raised more questions than it has answered. Its tight focus has provided information of a very specific nature about foreign news selection in three regional newspapers in France, Britain and the United States. Because of this tightness of focus, and also because of the study's lack of representativeness, its findings cannot be generalized, but they do suggest other avenues of research. It is also felt that the method of inquiry developed for this study—a combination of content analysis, participant observation and survey—is particularly appropriate for the exploration of these new avenues and the analysis of procedures and attitudes that are otherwise extremely difficult to gauge.

The study could be usefully extended to other regional newspapers, not only in France, Britain and the United States but also in other countries. Given sufficient time and/or manpower it might also be possible to use a random selection process, which would make the findings more generalizable. It would be particularly interesting to make a comparative analysis of newspapers in countries governed by different political systems or economic circumstances. A further step would be to extend the study to different types of newspapers, and, ultimately, to different media.

The same method could also be used to study other kinds of news content, in particular the coverage of national events, as well as the selection processes involved. And, here again, research could be extended to other media and other countries.

A number of such research projects, using the same methodology, would eventually yield valuable comparisons between different types and sizes of media in different countries and different cultural settings, and would greatly contribute to our understanding of news values and news selection processes. Repeated studies across time would also provide insights into changes taking place in journalistic procedures and management philosophies. Ultimately, it might even be possible to develop some kind of predictive framework linking certain kinds of structural and professional factors to certain types of journalistic output.

One unavoidable drawback to this line of inquiry, however, is that, while content analysis may be performed on data from identical time periods, observation must perforce take place at different time periods, at least if only one observer is used. The only real way to overcome this drawback would be to organize a large field study involving several groups of journalists in different news organizations in different countries, all making selections from the same day's news file.

For this study to be successful, several journalists belonging to the same news organization would have to work in the same setting and process the same news for the same edition or newscast. If the resulting news selections were widely divergent, then one might speculate that professional, cultural and organizational factors are less important than hitherto believed and that some other idiosyncratic factors are at work. If, on the other hand, news selections were seen to be similar within one organization but not between organizations, one could conclude that organizational factors are more important. Finally, if results were similar not only within organizations but also across organizations, while remaining dissimilar across countries, one could speculate that cultural forces were involved.

A study of this nature would certainly remove some of the controversies surrounding the vexed question of news values and would clear the way for much future research. However, it would be extremely difficult and costly to organize and would require the cooperation of researchers, the owners of news organizations, journalists and possibly labor unions in different countries.

Meanwhile, more realistically, further progress could be achieved by refining the taxonomy developed in Chapter 6 and applying it to a variety of different news selection situations. As has already been argued, most of the shortcomings of existing research in this area spring from the fact that the influences affecting the news selection process have been viewed as operating independently of one another. The advantage of the proposed taxonomy is that it enables the researcher to see how various groups of factors interact with one another. A further exploration of the causal paths involved might prove to be very fruitful. This particular taxonomy was developed for the selection of foreign news, but it is easy to see how it could be modified for the selection of national news, or even the gathering and editing processes associated with reporting.

Finally, this study has focused on foreign news content, which is determined almost exclusively by selection from wire services. Content analysis has shown very uniform foreign news coverage among regional newspapers and the wire services to which they subscribe, despite the continued existence of different journalistic images and traditions in the countries studied. Although these images and traditions are gradually fading under the influence of changing structural and professional factors, it is felt they must have *some* effect on journalistic processes. It has been seen that they have little impact on news topic selection. Perhaps they are reflected more in the way in which subjects are selected for reporting, in reportorial approaches, and in the actual writing of news stories. This suggests yet another line of research involving a semiotic or psycholinguistic approach, possibly within a cultural studies framework.

All in all, this study has confirmed the findings of some previous research, extended this research to other settings, broken some new ground with regard to the study of regional newspapers in different countries and added to our knowledge of journalistic practices and values by identifying a number of new factors influencing foreign news selection—especially image—and by exploring the relationship that exists among these factors. The fact that it has raised other questions and pointed to a number of interesting new avenues of investigation suggests that this field will continue to be a rich area of research for a long time to come.

ALTERNATIVE SOURCES OF MEDIA FUNDING

Meanwhile, as has been argued throughout this book, news coverage in the media as a whole, and in newspapers in particular, will probably continue to become more uniform. The main reason behind this growing uniformity is an increasing preoccupation with profit, brought about by changing patterns of ownership in a climate of intense competition. New management techniques, spurred by these changes, are modifying traditional journalistic images and procedures and creating a greater dependence on routine electronic sources.

This situation raises a number of questions about the purpose and usefulness of commercially owned and operated media vehicles in Western democracies. Is homogeneity of news coverage necessarily a bad thing, or must diversity be maintained at all costs? Is the delicate balance between the legitimate business objectives of the media and their duty to society in danger of disappearing? Can independent editorial opinion survive? Are our perceptions of the world being impoverished by mass-produced information? Can we allow profit to act as a gatekeeper in the news selection process?

These are questions of serious concern to all who believe in the importance of mass communication as a political, social and cultural catalyst, but they go far beyond the scope of this book and no attempt will be made to address them here. One question that should be addressed, however, is: What are the alternatives to commercially owned media? Without arguing—yet again—the pros and cons of various ideologically driven press systems,[1] it might be useful to review some of the media-funding alternatives that are open to us in a democratic society.

Government Subsidized Press

State intervention in press economics is viewed with horror in the United States, but this has not prevented the government from taking a hand to correct certain trends in the marketplace. As Robert Picard has argued, such intervention usually takes the form of taxation relief and preferential postal rates; indirect subsidies, in the shape of government advertising or bulk buying; and regulatory relief with regard to minimum wage and overtime requirements. Furthermore, the Newspaper Preservation Act has allowed some newspapers to engage in monopolistic practices that would not be allowed elsewhere and has encouraged growth through chain ownership. Government intervention may set out to be fair-minded but it in fact discourages independent ownership and reduces employment through the creation of economies of scale.[2]

Picard further argues that the purpose of state intervention should be to support plurality and the goals of a free press, a press that is for the public and not the media owners. To be succcesful, government aid must be direct, specific, selective and interventionistic. Such aid is common in many European countries, where it is seen as a way of limiting concentration of ownership and the loss of newspaper titles. It has been relatively successful in some cases but it has been powerless to prevent the empire building of such press magnates as Rupert Murdoch, Robert Maxwell and Robert Hersant. Historically, state intervention has been more successful in limiting the commercialization of the broadcast media in Europe, and the BBC remains a good example of what enlightened government action can achieve. However, increasing privatization and unclear intergovernmental media policies on the eve of European integration in 1992 leave a lot of uncertainty about the future status of broadcasting in Western Europe.[3]

In the United States, the question of government subsidies is moot. It is clear that, for constitutional reasons, any kind of state intervention, however well intentioned and however conducive to a better, more diversified, more balanced and more informative press, remains anathema. Paradoxically, in view of the dangers of commercialism and monopoly ownership described by Bagdikian,[4] the First Amendment may ultimately stand in the way of a truly free press.

Private Group Subsidies

Many of the same reservations held about government subsidies can be expressed with regard to subsidies from private interest groups. Usually, private interest groups have specific axes to grind and view the media as a convenient place to grind them. Frequently, they are able to air their views through their own privately owned publications. It would be most unusual for a private interest group to allocate subsidies to the media without expecting something in exchange, unless, of course, the primary objective of the group was to promote disinterested financing of the media. In any case, disinterested or not, there is unlikely ever to be a private interest group large enough to support a major media vehicle.

Advertising-free Press

Without advertising, the media would be free of some of the pressures brought by external businesss interests, but, assuming that owners continued to be motivated by profit, individual media would still have to compete for markets in order to exist. Most of the costs paid for by advertising would have to be passed on to the consumer, and this would make media usage prohibitively expensive. The result would be elite media reserved for those who could afford them, a situation somewhat similar to that of newspapers before the emergence of the penny press.[5]

Advertising-free broadcasting exists in many countries, but costs are not directly paid by the consumer. Funding may be provided by the government through some form of listening or viewing license, as is the case with the BBC and some other European broadcasting organizations. However, recent developments, such as the Peacock Report in Britain and the growing trend toward privatization, suggest that this form of funding may gradually disappear. Alternatively, the public may be asked to make voluntary donations, as with National Public Radio and the Public Broadcasting System, which also rely on corporate sponsorship, a form of disguised advertising. Even at its best, public broadcasting appeals only to a very small audience, and its future may be dependent on increased government support or wider corporate sponsorship, both of which have the potential of influencing programming.

Nonprofit Media

Nonprofit media are something of an anomaly in Western capitalist economies, but they do exist. Many associations publish newsletters, magazines, journals and other publications, usually limited to and supported by their membership, although they are not really news vehicles in the sense implied in this discussion. On the other hand, there are rare publications, such as the *Christian Science Monitor*, that are run along the lines of a nonprofit organization and yet contrive to provide a genuine news service of undisputed quality. Generally speaking, however, not only do they not make a profit, they usually run at a loss and this inevitably causes problems.

The *Monitor* has lost up to $15 million a year since the early 1960s, but these losses have been accepted by its publisher, The First Church of Christ, Scientist, because the paper has always been viewed as a public service of the church. In other words, the publication was subsidized by an organization whose members held enlightened ideas about the role and function of news vehicles. However, faced with dwindling membership and ever-increasing costs, the Christian Science Publishing Society completely revamped the newspaper in early 1989, reducing the number of pages, cutting back staff and closing down six of its foreign and domestic news bureaus.[6] This move followed an expansion of the organization's media activities into radio, a monthly magazine and television, which, together, had generated huge expenses.

There have also been many instances of losing newspapers being subsidized by other media in the same ownership group. In most cases the losing titles were not performing any major public service and could only be considered to be nonprofit by force of circumstance! In a few cases, though, truly worthy newspapers have been able to maintain their uncompromising dedication to the highest journalistic standards only because of ancillary activities in other fields. This has long been the case of the *New York Times*, which is run, to all intents and purposes, as a nonprofit enterprise.[7] One could hope that the increasing financial diversification of multimedia groups, described in Chapter 4, might produce similar situations, but recent developments in international media ownership suggest that this is highly unlikely.

Most people would agree that the alternative sources of media funding available to us are either unworkable or unacceptable in our present society. Consequently, we are left with the status quo: a commercially funded press system. Most self-respecting media vehicles are, of course, anxious to keep editorial decisions separate from commercial considerations, but the fact remains that the media are a business and that modern media managers are increasingly profit oriented. This is nothing new. Furthermore, not all media owners are crass capitalists. Many of them continue to have genuinely enlightened views about the role of the media. What is new, though, is that the technical innovations introduced by profit-conscious media management seem inevitably to be producing greater homogeneity of news content.

Journalism is already in a state of transition. As we move through the 1990s, and as even more technical innovations are introduced, further change is likely. What will probably emerge are two forms of journalism, two distinct "ideal types"—in the Weberian sense of the term. First, an increasingly profit-oriented journalism, based on multimedia ownership, in which homogenized news is seen as a vehicle for advertising. Second, an information-based journalism, supported by owners and managers who continue to believe that the media have a responsibility toward society and that diversity of coverage and opinion are an essential feature of that responsibility.

Perhaps the future of journalism lies somewhere between these two "ideal types." Already an artificial intelligence-assisted newspaper management system has proved itself capable of routinizing nearly 80 percent of news and advertising production decisions.[8] Although the developers of this system have gone out of business, it is only a matter of time before radical new technologies of this kind are adopted. It is to be hoped that they will be accompanied by a measure of social responsibility. The term *social responsibility* has been used and abused so much that it has almost lost its meaning—almost, but not quite. Although it has had its detractors,[9] it is a concept that is as viable today as when the Hutchins Commission recommended it as a remedy for "meaninglessness, flatness, distortion and the perpetuation of misunderstanding."[10] If these new technologies are indeed utilized with a sense of responsibility, the savings in time realized should give journalists the freedom to do what they do best: select, edit and interpret the news. As long as we care about the freedoms of the society in which we live, we must continue to take an interest in who is choosing the news.

NOTES

1. Siebert, Peterson and Schramm, *Four Theories of the Press*; William A. Hachten, *The World News Prism: Changing Media, Clashing Ideologies*, 2d ed. (Ames: Iowa State University Press, 1987); Altschull, *Agents of Power*.

2. Robert G. Picard, "State Intervention in U.S. Press Economics," *Gazette* 30 (1982), pp. 3–11.

3. Denis McQuail and Karen Siune, *New Media Politics: Comparative Perspectives in Western Europe* (London: Sage Publications, 1986).

4. Bagdikian, *The Media Monopoly*.

5. For an excellent recent discussion of the penny press, see John C. Nerone, "The Mythology of the Penny Press," *Critical Studies in Mass Communication* 4 (December 1987), pp. 376–404, and critical responses by Michael Schudson, Dan Schiller, Donald Shaw and John Pauly.

6. Stephen J. Simurda, "Can the Stripped-down *Monitor* Stay A-float?" *Columbia Journalism Review* (March/April 1989), pp. 42–45.

7. Irving Kristol, "The Underdeveloped Profession," *The Public Interest* 2 (Winter 1967), pp. 36–52.

8. Melvin L. DeFleur and Everette E. Dennis, *Understanding Mass Communication*, 3d ed. (Boston: Houghton Mifflin, 1988), p. 246.

9. John C. Merrill, *The Imperative of Freedom* (New York: Hastings House, 1974); Altschull, *Agents of Power*, see Appendix "The Absurdity of Social Responsibility," pp. 301–305.

10. Commission on Freedom of the Press, *A Free and Responsible Press* (Chicago: University of Chicago Press, 1947).

APPENDIX I

METHODOLOGICAL NOTE

From the outset of this study, the researcher's intention to compare the foreign news coverage of newspapers dictated the use of systematic content analysis. The need to understand the influences affecting news content, many of which cannot be measured by empirical means, suggested participant observation as an appropriate method of inquiry. Finally, simple survey questionnaires were used not only because they provide answers to direct questions, but also because they lend some structure to what might otherwise appear to be an unstructured research design. This methodological note discusses some of the technical aspects of the research methods used.

GENERAL

Taken individually, each of the research methods used raises problems of external validity, mainly because the phenomena being studied are very specific. It is obvious that the content analysis of one regional newspaper in a given country is not going to produce widely representative results. Nor can the observation of a small number of journalists within a newspaper newsroom produce data applicable to other kinds of journalism. Also, without a large random sample, the survey questionnaires used in the study cannot yield any generalizable findings.

However, although these are genuine problems, the nature of the study is such that too much emphasis should not be placed on them. Its purpose is less to find points of similarity within national media systems than to establish means of comparison among certain types of journalism in different countries.

Consequently, a great deal has been done to maximize *internal* validity. For example, as discussed in Chapter 5, the newspapers were carefully selected to make sure that they were similar in relative size, type, structure, level and readership. Observation was limited to only those journalists engaged in the selection of foreign news. Furthermore, in order to check on whether those particular journalists might be relatively typical, observation and interviews were extended to other newspapers. Interviews followed set patterns in each newspaper, while the questions used in the survey were of course identical. Finally, the categories used in the content analysis were developed with some rigor.

The time period used for content analysis, May 4–15, 1987, was selected with some care so as to avoid important seasonal events or holiday periods likely to skew news content or affect newsroom staffing. The periods chosen for observation were selected more arbitrarily, as a function of possible travel schedules, but care was also taken to avoid major holiday periods for the same reasons as those given above. May 25 to June 5, 1987, was spent at *Le Courier de l'Ouest*, June 15 to 26, 1987, was spent at the *Eastern Daily Press*, and May 23 to June 3, 1988, was spent at the Evansville *Courier*.

The length of the period selected for content analysis was determined partly by the volume of work it would generate and partly by its appropriateness as a sample. Stempel has argued that any period of four days or more will adequately represent the news pattern in a media system,[1] so a period of two weeks, which produced 2,727 news items for analysis, was thought to be more than adequate. The length of the periods selected for observation was governed mainly by financial considerations, but it was also felt that two weeks were long enough to overcome most of the bias produced by the presence of an observer in the newsroom, and short enough to preserve the researcher's objectivity by avoiding a tendency to "go native," a common phenomenon in observational studies.

CONTENT ANALYSIS

Several aspects of the content analysis performed for this study require discussion.

Categories and Definitions

The subject categories selected for content analysis were developed from the topics used in the Foreign Images study undertaken for

UNESCO by the International Association for Mass Communication Research.[2] They are as follows:

- Diplomatic or political activity between states. For the purposes of this study, only activities of *foreign* states reported from a foreign location were considered.
- Internal political conflict or crisis in a foreign country. The Iran-contra affair, although it involved arms deals and hostage negotiations, was placed in this category because its implications threatened political stability within the United States.
- Elections, election results, election campaigns; government changes resulting from elections or routine reshuffles.
- Other political activities, including parliamentary procedures and debates, and legislative matters.
- Armed conflict or the threat of armed conflict. This could include actual fighting or the deployment of troops in a threatening way.
- Peace moves or peace negotiations, as distinct from routine diplomatic activities.
- Military expenditure, arms deals, new weapons or weapon tests, military bases, and military exercises.
- Agreements on trade, including bilateral or multilateral talks or legislation on tariffs, customs, etc.
- International trade, giving details of actual transactions, trade figures, or import-export levels.
- Economic performance, domestic trade figures, and industrial output.
- Prices of goods as they affect cost of living.
- Industrial projects, such as new manufacturing installations or processes.
- Agricultural matters, including crop production, crop damage and climatic conditions, but excluding agricultural prices likely to affect cost of living.
- Industrial disputes such as strikes, and labor unrest, as distinct from civil unrest.
- Monetary matters and exchange rates, including news affecting stock markets but excluding standard stock market reports.
- Energy, including production and consumption figures.
- Disaster and famine relief, reported either from the country granting relief or the country receiving it.
- Military aid, either in the form of financial aid for the purchase of military equipment, or the supply of military equipment itself.
- Other aid, including aid in the form of financial assistance or personnel, but excluding military aid or disaster relief.
- Social problems. Drug taking and drug addiction are included in this category, but drug-related medical conditions such as AIDS are not.
- Crime and police matters. This category includes violent and white-collar crime as well as drug-related incidents in which the criminal aspect is more important than the social aspect.
- Air crashes and accidents, including public transit accidents, and industrial accidents involving injury or loss of life, but not toxic waste or chemical leakages.

- Culture and the arts, including museums, exhibitions and the performance of "serious" music, as distinct from "entertainment."
- Religion, including church news, doctrinal matters, and news of the Pope.
- Scientific and medical news, including reports on AIDS and AIDS research.
- Entertainment and entertainers, as distinct from "serious" artists and performances.
- Sport, including items on sports celebrities or sport as an activity, but excluding sports results.
- Human interest and the bizarre. This category may include certain crime stories if their human interest aspect is more important than their criminal aspect.
- Civil unrest, including demonstrations or riots unconnected with labor disputes, as well as news about dissidents.
- Environment and pollution. This category includes toxic waste scares, spillages and items about acid rain or the ozone layer.
- Natural disasters, including earthquakes, floods, droughts, hurricanes, etc.
- Terrorism. This includes not only acts of terrorism, but also antiterrorist police action, extradition proceedings or trials.
- Other.

The above categories proved to be not only mutually exclusive, but also very comprehensive. Indeed, only 0.4 percent of all the items coded were placed in the Other category.

Prominence

The newspaper items analyzed were also coded for prominence using a scale adapted from Richard Budd's "attention score," originally developed for a study of Australian and New Zealand newspapers.[3] Briefly, Budd allocated one point for each of the following criteria:

- An item with a headline two columns or more in width.
- An item with a headline occupying more than half the number of columns of the page.
- An item appearing above the fold of any page.
- An item occupying three-fourths of a column or more.
- An item appearing on page one, the editorial page or the sports page.

Thus any one item could receive an attention score ranging from zero to five points depending on how and where the article was played.

This system, although useful for Budd's study, was thought to be inappropriate for foreign news coverage in regional newspapers, in which foreign news items tend to be very short and restricted to columns of world briefs. It was felt, however, that Budd's basic approach was sound and that his "attention score" could be neatly adapted for the purposes of this study. Consequently, all newspaper items were given one point for each of the following criteria:

- An item appearing on the front page.
- An item appearing above the fold on the front page.
- An item containing more than three paragraphs.
- An item appearing with a photograph.
- An item appearing across two or more columns.

News items were, therefore, given a prominence rating of from zero to five points. As in Budd's research, this device made it possible to distinguish differences of emphasis among the three newspapers studied, whereas straightforward category analysis showed very little variation.

Violence and Origin

In order to replicate previous studies, all items were also coded for violence and origin. For the purposes of this study, violent news items were defined as those in which death or injury was caused as the result of conflict. Potentially violent situations, such as confrontations between police and strikers, were not coded as violent unless actual physical injury ensued.

In this study, the definition of origin was limited to whether a story originated in a northern or a southern hemisphere country. Once again, recourse was had to the UNESCO Foreign Images study, which included a list of less-developed and more-developed countries.[4] Generally speaking, this classification follows the logic behind the 1975 North-South Conference in Paris.

Northern countries include: Australia, Austria, Belgium, Canada, Czechoslovakia, Denmark, France, Germany (Democratic Republic), Germany (Federal Republic), Greece, Hungary, Ireland, Italy, Japan, Norway, Poland, Portugal, South Africa, Spain, Sweden, Switzerland, United Kingdom, United States, USSR, Vatican City. Southern countries are represented by sixty-six less-developed countries, including Africa (minus South Africa), Asia (minus the eastern USSR), South America, and Oceania (minus Australia).

Intercoder Reliability

For linguistic reasons, it was not possible to perform an intercoder reliability check, and, in fact, all the coding was done by the same person. However, the categories used were very similar to those developed for the Foreign Images study, which reported a Scott's pi in the region of 0.7 to 0.8 for topic classification. In the opinion of the reporters of the UNESCO study, the reliability of coding was "certainly high enough for the overall pattern of results to be confidently accepted as meaningful, particularly in view of the large number of items covered by the analysis."[5]

PARTICIPANT OBSERVATION

Participant observation raises problems of external validity and observer bias, particularly with a single observer. There is little doubt, however, that it is the only suitable research method for the study of such an internalized process as news selection. It has already been argued that external validity is not of prime importance in this study, which is more concerned with understanding than predicting. Furthermore, the problem of observer bias can be largely avoided by taking appropriate precautions.

Lincoln and Guba have laid out a whole paradigm of "naturalistic inquiry," and many of their methods proved to be useful in designing, planning and implementing this study.[6] The researcher had already established "prior ethnography" from years of familiarity with the media systems of the three countries studied. He also took great care to create a climate of "trust" by visiting the observation sites well in advance of actual data collection. He made use of flexible "working hypotheses," thus avoiding some of the dangers of preconceived theoretical positions. He used "persistent observation," which adds a dimension of salience to what otherwise might be considered a sea of mindless detail. During interviews, data were recorded by handwritten notes rather than a tape machine, which tends to cause "respondent distrust." Finally, summary notes were written up periodically so as to pinpoint salient trends or isolated phenomena, and also to "fine tune" working hypotheses.

Interviews were of two types. Sixteen interviews were conducted with journalists responsible for foreign news selection. These tended to be very informal, more akin to friendly chats. The fact that the researcher was often viewed more as a fellow journalist than an academic seemed to make these talks very candid. It was felt that structured questions would introduce an air of formality that might inhibit frankness. It was usually more informative to let the interviewee ramble on at will than try to keep him/her within a set structure. This was time-consuming and generated a mass of data that had to be reduced at a later stage, but the results were satisfying.

Fourteen interviews were conducted with editors, either at the newspapers observed or at those newspapers that were visited only briefly. These interviews were more structured, partly to provide more focus, but also because of time constraints. Apart from general "warm-up" questions about the history of the newspaper, its ownership, circulation, and staffing, editors were asked to comment, at some stage during the interview, on the following:

- recent developments in regional newspapers
- how these developments have affected:
  production
  circulation
  layout
  editorial procedures
- level of computerization within the newspaper
- the effect of electronic news management systems on editorial procedures
- the effect of ownership on editorial procedures

Here, again, while comments on these topics were always invited, it was useful to allow the interviewee to broach other topics and talk at will. For this reason, questions were always framed in an open-ended way.

SURVEY

The survey questionnaire used was basically very straightforward. A copy of it is to be found at the end of this note. The only real difficulty encountered was framing the questions in such a way that they could be translated to a different language, or culture, without losing any of their meaning. A further difficulty was the fact that the notion of "ranking" did not appear to be fully understood by the British and French respondents, despite what were thought to be very clear instructions.

QUESTIONNAIRE

1) Newspaper _____

2) Circulation _____

3) Total number of journalists _____

4) Number of journalists on foreign news _____

5) Name of person answering the questionnaire _____

6) Job description _____

7) Do you ever select foreign news? _____

8) If so, how often? _____

9) Number of years in profession _____

10) Number of years with this newspaper _____

11) Previous newspapers, if any _____

12) What journalism training have you had? _____

13) Where did you receive it? _____

14) Do you have a university degree? _____

15) If so, in what? _____

16) Have you taken any other kind of specialized training?

If so, please specify _____

17) What qualities do you look for when selecting a news
item from a wire service? Please circle Yes or No:

			Ranking (see below)
- accuracy	Yes	No	_____
- how topical	Yes	No	_____
- local impact	Yes	No	_____
- right length	Yes	No	_____
- human interest	Yes	No	_____
- byline (author)	Yes	No	_____
- geographic origin	Yes	No	_____
- other	Yes	No	_____

If "other" please specify _____

Please rank the qualities listed above. Put 1 next to the
most important, 2 next to the next most important, etc.

18) What features would make you reject a news item? _____

_____

19) What qualities do you look for when selecting a <u>foreign</u>
news item? Please circle Yes or No:

			Ranking (see below)
- accuracy	Yes	No	_____
- how topical	Yes	No	_____
- local impact	Yes	No	_____
- right length	Yes	No	_____
- human interest	Yes	No	_____
- byline (author)	Yes	No	_____
- geographic origin	Yes	No	_____
- other	Yes	No	_____

If "other" please specify _____

Please rank the qualities listed above. Put 1 next to the
most important, 2 next to the next most important, etc.

20) What features would make you reject a <u>foreign</u> news

item? _____

21) Below are several factors that may guide your selection
of news. Please try to rank them, putting 1 next to the
factor you consider the most important, 2 next to the next
most important, etc.

			Ranking
- general editorial policy	Yes	No	_____
- professional training	Yes	No	_____
- immediate supervisor	Yes	No	_____
- fellow journalists	Yes	No	_____
- personal convictions	Yes	No	_____
- readers´ interest	Yes	No	_____
- other	Yes	No	_____

If "other" please specify _____

_____

22) Finally, how would you define "news"? _____

_____

_____

THANK YOU FOR YOUR COOPERATION. IT IS GREATLY APPRECIATED.

NOTES

1. Guido H. Stempel III, "Sample Size for Classifying Subject Matter in Dailies," *Journalism Quarterly* 29:2 (Summer 1952), pp. 333–334.

2. Sreberny-Mohammadi et al., "Foreign News in the Media."

3. Budd, "Attention Score."

4. Sreberny-Mohammadi et al., "Foreign News in the Media," pp. 88–89.

5. Ibid., p. 15.

6. Yvonna S. Lincoln and Egon G. Guba, *Naturalistic Inquiry* (Beverly Hills, Calif.: Sage, 1985).

APPENDIX II

JOURNALISTIC CODES

United States

American Society of Newspaper Editors
A STATEMENT OF PRINCIPLES
Preamble

The First Amendment, protecting freedom of expression from abridgement by any law, guarantees to the people through their press a constitutional right, and thereby places on newspaper people a particular responsibility.

Thus journalism demands of its practitioners not only industry and knowledge but also the pursuit of a standard of integrity proportionate to the journalist's singular obligation.

To this end the American Society of Newspaper Editors sets forth this Statement of Principles as a standard encouraging the highest ethical and professional performance.

Article I—Responsibility

The primary purpose of gathering and distributing news and opinion is to serve the general welfare by informing the people and enabling them to make judgments on the issues of the time. Newspapermen and women who abuse the power of their professional role for selfish motives or unworthy purposes are faithless to that public trust.

The American press was made free not just to inform or just to serve as a forum for debate but also to bring an independent scrutiny to bear on the forces of power in society, including the conduct of official power at all levels of government.

Article II—Freedom of the Press

Freedom of the press belongs to the people. It must be defended against encroachment or assault from any quarter, public or private.

Journalists must be constantly alert to see that the public's business is conducted in public. They must be vigilant against all who would exploit the press for selfish purposes.

Article III—Independence

Journalists must avoid impropriety and the appearance of impropriety as well as any conflict of interest or the appearance of conflict. They should neither accept anything nor pursue any activity that might compromise or seem to compromise their integrity.

Article IV—Truth and Accuracy

Good faith with the reader is the foundation of good journalism. Every effort must be made to assure that the news content is accurate, free from bias and in context, and that all sides are presented fairly. Editorials, analytical articles and commentary should be held to the same standards of accuracy with respect to facts as news reports.

Significant errors of fact, as well as errors of omission, should be corrected promptly and prominently.

Article V—Impartiality

To be impartial does not require the press to be unquestioning or to refrain from editorial expression. Sound practice, however, demands a clear distinction for the reader between news reports and opinion. Articles that contain opinion or personal interpretation should be clearly identified.

Article VI—Fair Play

Journalists should respect the rights of people involved in the news, observe the common standards of decency and stand accountable to the public for the fairness and accuracy of their news reports.

Persons publicly accused should be given the earliest opportunity to respond.

Pledges of confidentiality to news sources must be honored at all costs, and therefore should not be given lightly. Unless there is a clear and pressing need to maintain confidences, sources of information should be identified.

These principles are intended to preserve, protect and strengthen the bond of trust and respect between American journalists and the American people, a bond that is essential to sustain the grant of freedom entrusted to both by the nation's founders.

United Kingdom

National Union of Journalists
CODE OF PROFESSIONAL CONDUCT

1. A journalist has a duty to maintain the highest professional and ethical standards.

2. A journalist shall at all times defend the principle of the freedom of the press and other media in relation to the collection of information and the expression of comment and criticism. He/she shall strive to eliminate distortion, news suppression and censorship.

3. A journalist shall strive to ensure that the information he/she disseminates is fair and accurate, avoid the expression of comment and conjecture as established fact, and falsification by distortion, selection or misrepresentation.

4. A journalist shall rectify promptly any harmful inaccuracies, ensure that correction and apologies receive due prominence and afford the right of reply to persons criticized when the issue is of sufficient importance.

5. A journalist shall obtain information, photographs and illustrations only by straightforward means. The use of other means can be justified only by over-riding considerations of the public interest. The journalist is entitled to exercise a personal conscientious objection to the use of such means.

6. Subject to justification by over-riding considerations of the public interest, a journalist shall do nothing which entails intrusion into private grief and distress.

7. A journalist shall protect confidential sources of information.

8. A journalist shall not accept bribes nor shall he/she allow other inducements to influence the performance of his/her professional duties.

9. A journalist shall not lend himself/herself to the distortion or suppression of the truth because of advertising or other considerations.

10. A journalist shall neither originate nor process material which encourages discrimination on grounds of race, colour, creed, gender or sexual orientation.

11. A journalist shall not take private advantage of information gained in the course of his/her duties, before the information is public knowledge.

12. A journalist shall not by way of statement, voice or appearance endorse by advertisements any commercial product or service save for the promotion of his/her work or of the medium by which he/she is employed.

France

CHARTER OF THE PROFESSIONAL DUTIES OF FRENCH JOURNALISTS
(This is a translation from the French text, which is to be found on the following page)

A journalist worthy of the name:

—assumes responsibility for everything he/she writes;

—considers libel, groundless accusations, the falsification of documents, the distortion of facts, and untruths to be the most serious professional misconduct;

—recognizes only the jurisdiction of his/her peers, who are sovereign with respect to professional honor;

· —accepts only those duties that are compatible with his/her professional dignity;

—refrains from using false titles or qualifications, and from using dishonest means to obtain information or to mislead an informant;

—does not accept money in a public service or a private enterprise in which his/her journalist's status, influence or contacts may be exploited;

—refuses to sign articles promoting commercial or financial interests;

—does not plagiarize;

—always cites colleagues whose materials he/she borrows;
—does not solicit the position of a colleague, or encourage the termination of his/her employment by offering to work for less money;
—maintains professional secrecy;
—does not exploit freedom of the press for lucrative purposes;
—defends the right to publish honestly his/her stories;
—holds scrupulousness and the respect for justice to be primary qualities;
—does not confuse his/her role with that of the police.

France

CHARTE DES DEVOIRS PROFESSIONNELS DES JOURNALISTES FRANCAIS

Un journaliste digne de ce nom:

—prend la responsabilité de tous ses écrits;
—tient la calomnie, les accusations sans preuves, l'altération des documents, la déformation des faits, le mensonge, pour les plus graves fautes profession-nelles;
—ne reconnaît que la juridiction de ses pairs, souverains en matière d'honneur professionnnel;
—n'accepte que des missions compatibles avec sa dignité professionnelle;
—s'interdit d'invoquer un titre ou une qualité imaginaires, d'user de moyens déloyaux, pour obtenir une information ou surprendre la bonne foi de qui-conque;
—ne touche pas d'argent dans un service public ou une entreprise privée où sa qualité de journaliste, ses influences, ses relations soient susceptibles d'être exploitées;
—ne signe pas de son nom des articles de réclame commerciale ou financière;
—ne commet aucun plagiat;
—cite les confrères dont il reproduit un texte quelconque;
—ne sollicite pas la place d'un confrère ni ne provoque son renvoi en offrant de travailler à des conditions inférieures;
—garde la secret professionnel;
—n'use pas de la liberté de la presse dans une intention intéressée;
—revendique la liberté de publier honnêtement ses informations;
—tient le scrupule et le souci de la justice pour des règles premières;
—ne confond pas son role avec celui du policier.

BIBLIOGRAPHY

Albert, Pierre. *La presse française*. Paris: La Documentation Française, 1978.

Albert, Pierre, and Fernand Terrou. *Histoire de la presse*. Fourth Edition. Paris: P.U.F., 1985.

Altschull, J. Herbert. *Agents of Power: The Role of the News Media in Human Affairs*. New York: Longman, 1984.

American Society of Newspaper Editors. "A Statement of Principles." October 23, 1975.

Archambault, François, and Jean-François Lemoîne. *Quatre milliards de journaux*. Paris: Alain Moreau, 1977.

Atwood, L.E., and S.J. Bullion. "News Maps of the World: A View from Asia." In *International Perspectives on the News*, edited by L.E. Atwood and S.M Murphy. Carbondale: Southern Illinois University Press, 1982.

Bagdikian, Ben. *The Information Machines: Their Impact on Men and the Media*. New York: Harper and Row, 1971.

———."Woodstein U: Notes on the Mass Production and Questionable Education of Journalists." *Atlantic* 239:2 (1977): 81–92.

———. *The Media Monopoly*. Second Edition. Boston: Beacon Press, 1987.

Bainbridge, Cyril. *One Hundred Years of Journalism: Social Aspects of the Press*. London: Macmillan, 1984.

Balle, Francis. "Communication Revolution and Freedom of Expression." In *The Media Revolution in America and Western Europe*, edited by Everett Rogers and Francis Balle. Norwood, N.J.: Ablex, 1985.

Becker, Lee, Jeffrey Fruit and Susan Caudill, with Sharon Dunwoody and Leonard Tipton. *The Training and Hiring of Journalists*. Norwood, N.J.: Ablex, 1987.

Bellanger, Claude, Jacques Godechot, Pierre Guiral and Fernand Terrou. *Histoire générale de la presse française*. Paris: P.U.F., 1976.

Bertrand, Claude-Jean, and Miguel Urabayen. "European Mass Media in the 1980s." In *The Media Revolution in America and Western Europe*, edited by Everett Rogers and Francis Balle. Norwood, N.J.: Ablex, 1985.

Besson, Alain. *La presse locale en liberté surveillée*. Paris: Les Editions Ouvrières, 1977.

Bogart, Leo. *Press and Public: Who Reads What, When, Where and Why in American Newspapers*. Hillsdale, N.J.: Lawrence Erlbaum Associates, 1981.

Bohère, Georges. *Profession: Journalist*. Geneva: ILO, 1984.

Boyce, George, James Curran and Pauline Wingate. *Newspaper History from the Seventeenth Century to the Present Day*. London: Constable, 1978.

Boyd-Barrett, Oliver. *The International News Agencies*. London: Constable, 1980.

Brannigan, Colin. "Training: The Greatest Problem Facing the Industry." In *The British Press*. London: The Commonwealth Press Union, 1981.

Brants, Kees. "Policing the Cable." In *New Media Politics: Comparative Perspectives in Western Europe*, edited by Denis McQuail and Karen Siune, pp. 55–56. London: Sage Publications, 1986.

Breed, Warren. "Social Control in the Newsroom: A Functional Analysis." *Social Forces* 33 (1955): 325–335.

Budd, Richard W. "Attention Score: A Device for Measuring News Play." *Journalism Quarterly* 41:2 (Spring 1964): 259–262.

Cayrol, Roland. *L'ORTF face aux élections de mars 1973: une étude d'observation du service politique de la première chaîne de télévision française*. Strasbourg: European Political Consortium for Political Research, 1974.

Censer, Jack R., and Jeremy D. Popkin. *Press and Politics in Pre-Revolutionary France*. Berkeley: University of California Press, 1987.

Clark, Peter. *Sixteen Million Readers: Evening Newspapers in the U.K.* London: Holt, Rinehart and Winston, 1981.

Christian, Harry. "Journalists' Occupational Ideologies and Press Commercialization." In *The Sociology of Journalism and the Press*, edited by Harry Christian. Monograph 29. Keele: University of Keele, 1980.

Cleverly, Graham. *The Fleet Street Disaster: British National Newspapers as a Case Study in Mismanagement.* London: Constable, 1976.

Cohen, Stanley, and Jock Young. *The Manufacture of News.* London: Constable, 1973.

Commission on Freedom of the Press. *A Free and Responsible Press.* Chicago: University of Chicago Press, 1947.

Compaine, Benjamin M. *The Newspaper Industry in the 1980s: An Assessment of Economics and Technology.* White Plains, N.Y.: Knowledge Industry Publications, 1980.

Compaine, Benjamin M. et al. *Who Owns the Media? Concentration of Ownership in the Mass Communications Industry.* Second Edition. White Plains, N.Y.: Knowledge Industry Publications, 1982.

Curran, James, and Jean Seaton. *Power Without Responsibility: The Press and Broadcasting in Britain.* Second Edition. London: Methuen, 1985.

Dajani, N., and J. Donohue. "Foreign News in the Arab Press: A Content Analysis." *Gazette* 19:3 (1973): 154–170.

DeFleur, Melvin L., and Everette E. Dennis. *Understanding Mass Communication.* Third Edition. Boston: Houghton Mifflin, 1988.

Dennis, Everette E. "Journalism Education: Failing Grades from a Dean." *ASNE Bulletin.* October 1983.

Derieux, Emmanuel. *La presse quotidienne française.* Paris: Armand Colin, 1974.

Dodge, John. "An Overdue Partnership." In *The British Press,* pp. 70–71. London: The Commonwealth Press Union, 1981.

Dow Jones Newspaper Fund. *1988 Journalism Career and Scholarship Guide.* Princeton, N.J.: Dow Jones Newspaper Fund, 1988.

Dreier, Peter, and Steve Weinberg. "Interlocking Directorates." *Columbia Journalism Review* (November–December 1979): 51–68.

Emery, Edwin, and Michael Emery. *The Press and America: An Interpretive History of the Mass Media.* Sixth Edition. Englewood Cliffs, N.J.: Prentice-Hall, 1988.

Ettema, James S., and D. Charles Whitney. *Individuals in Mass Media Organizations: Creativity and Constraint.* Beverly Hills, Calif.: Sage, 1982.

Fishman, Mark. *Manufacturing the News.* Austin: University of Texas Press, 1980.

Freiberg, J.W. *The French Press: Class, State and Ideology.* New York: Praeger, 1981.

Future Committee. *Communications 1990.* Columbia: School of Journalism, University of Columbia-Missouri, 1980.

Galtung, Johan, and Mari H. Ruge. "The Structure of Foreign News." *Journal of Peace Research* 2:1 (1965): 64–91.

Gans, Herbert J. *Deciding What's News: A Study of CBS Evening News, NBC Nightly News, Newsweek and Time*. New York: Vintage Books, 1980.

Gaunt, Philip. "Image Versus Ideology: A Further Step Toward a Theory of News Content Based on a Comparative Study of French and British Newspapers." Presented at the 14th Annual Conference of the Midwest Association for Public Opinion Research, Chicago, November 18–19, 1988.

Gerbner, George, and George Marvanyi. "The Many Worlds of the World's Press." *Journal of Communication* 27:1 (Winter 1977): 52–66.

Gitlin, Todd. *The Whole World is Watching*. Berkeley: University of California Press, 1980.

Golding, Peter, and Philip Elliott. *Making the News*. London: Longman, 1979.

Grant, Moyra. *The British Media*. London: Comedia, 1984.

Gray, Richard G., and G. Cleveland Wilhoit. "Portrait of the U.S. Journalist, 1982–1983." Presented to the American Society of Newspaper Editors Convention, Denver, Colorado, May 9, 1983.

Guillou, Bernard. *Les groupes multimédias de communication*. Paris: La Documentation Française, 1984.

Gurevitch, Michael, and Jay Blumler. "The Construction of Election News: An Observation Study at the BBC." In *Individuals in Mass Media Organizations*, edited by James S. Ettema and D. Charles Whitney, pp. 179–204. Beverly Hills, Calif.: Sage, 1982.

Hachten, William A. *The World News Prism: Changing Media, Clashing Ideologies*. Second Edition. Ames: Iowa State University Press, 1987.

Haquin, Bénédicte. "Les entreprises de presse: des employeurs insatisfaits." *Presse-Actualité* (June-July 1985): 24.

Harris, Michael, and Alan J. Lee. *The Press in English Society from the Seventeenth to the Nineteenth Centuries*. Rutherford, N.J.: Fairleigh Dickinson University Press, 1986.

Hartley, Nicholas, Peter Gudgeon and Rosemary Crafts. *Concentration of Ownership in the Provincial Press*. London: HMSO for the Royal Commission on the Press, 1977.

Hernett, Isabelle. "Les écoles de communication." *EPP* (June 16, 1986): 60–64.

Hester, Al. "Theoretical Considerations in Predicting Volume and Direction of International Information Flow." *Gazette* 19:4 (1973): 239–247.

Hirsch, Paul M. "Occupational, Organizational, and Institutional

Models in Mass Media Research: Toward an Integrated Framework." In *Strategies for Communication Research*, edited by Paul M. Hirsch, Peter V. Miller and F. Gerald Kline. Beverly Hills, Calif.: Sage, 1977.

Hirsch, Paul M., Peter V. Miller and F. Gerald Kline. *Strategies for Communication Research*. Beverly Hills, Calif.: Sage, 1977.

Hollingsworth, Mark. *The Press and Political Dissent: A Question of Censorship*. London: Pluto Press, 1986.

Hunter, Frederic N. "Grub Street and Academia: The Relationship between Journalism and Education, 1880–1940." Ph.D. Dissertation, City University, London, 1984.

Hur, K. Kyoon. "A Critical Analysis of International News Flow Research." *Critical Studies in Mass Communication* 1 (1984): 365–378.

Hynds, Ernest. *American Newspapers in the 1980s*. New York: Hastings House, 1980.

Jackson, Ian. *The Provincial Press and the Community*. Manchester: Manchester University Press, 1971.

Johnstone, John W.C., Edward J. Slawski and William D. Bowman. "The Professional Values of American Newsmen." *Public Opinion Quarterly* 36:4 (Winter 1972–73): 522–540.

Katzen, May. *Mass Communication: Teaching and Studies at Universities*. Paris: UNESCO Press, 1975.

Kristol, Irving. "The Underdeveloped Profession." *The Public Interest* 2 (Winter 1967): 36–52.

Kurian, George T. *World Press Encyclopedia*. New York: Facts on File, 1982.

Lent, John A. "Foreign News in American Media." *Journal of Communication* 27:1 (Winter 1977): 46–51.

Lestroha, Patrice. "Les gros poissons, la friture et les requins." *L'Evénement du jeudi* (January 21–27, 1988): 8–10.

Lincoln, Yvonna S., and Egon G. Guba. *Naturalistic Inquiry*. Beverly Hills, Calif.: Sage, 1985.

Lohr, Steve. "Britain's Maverick Mogul." *The New York Times Magazine* (May 1, 1988): 52 et seq.

MacLeod, Alexander. "New Technology, Avid Readers Kindle Renaissance for British Newspapers." *Christian Science Monitor* (November 20, 1988): 12.

Masmoudi, Mustapha. "The New World Information Order." *Journal of Communication* 29:2 (Spring 1979): 172–185.

Mathien, Michel. *La presse quotidienne régionale*. Second Edition. Paris: P.U.F., 1986.

Mazzoleni, Gianpetro. "Mass Telematics: Facts and Fiction." In *New*

Media Politics: Comparative Perspectives in Western Europe, edited by Denis McQuail and Karen Siune, pp. 100–114. London: Sage Publications, 1986.

McCombs, Maxwell E., and Donald L. Shaw. "The Agenda-Setting Function of Mass Media." *Public Opinion Quarterly* 36 (Summer 1972): 176–187.

McQuail, Denis. *Analysis of Newspaper Content*. London: HMSO, 1977.

McQuail, Denis, and Karen Siune. *New Media Politics: Comparative Perspectives in Western Europe*. London: Sage Publications, 1986.

Merrill, John C. *The Imperative of Freedom*. New York: Hastings House, 1974.

————.*Global Journalism: A Survey of the World's Mass Media*. New York: Longman, 1983.

Mott, Frank Luther. *American Journalism, A History: 1690–1960*. Third Edition. New York: Macmillan, 1982.

Mountjoy, Peter Roger. "The Working Class Press and Working Class Conservatism." In *Newspaper History from the Seventeenth Century to the Present Day*, edited by George Boyce, James Curran and Pauline Wingate. London: Constable, 1978.

National Council for the Training of Journalists. *Newspaper Journalism Syllabus: Aims*. London: National Council for the Training of Journalists, May 1984.

Newspaper Society, The. *Training for Newspaper Journalism*. London: The Newspaper Society, n.d.

Picard, Robert. "State Intervention in U.S. Press Economics." *Gazette* 30 (1982): 3–11.

Popkin, Jeremy D. *The Right-Wing Press in France, 1792–1800*. Chapel Hill: University of North Carolina Press, 1980.

————."The *Gazette de Leyde* and French Politics under Louis XVI." In *Press and Politics in Pre-Revolutionary France*, edited by Jack R. Censer and Jeremy D. Popkin. Berkeley: University of California Press, 1987.

Porter, Henry. *Lies, Damned Lies and Some Exclusives*. London: Chatto and Windus, 1984.

Powell, Bill. "Murdoch's Empire." *Newsweek* (August 22, 1988): 42–43.

Project on the Future of Journalism and Mass Communications Education. *Planning for Curricular Change*. Eugene: School of Journalism, University of Oregon, 1984.

Richstad, Jim, and Michael A. Anderson. *Crisis in International News: Policies and Prospects*. New York: Columbia University Press, 1981.

Righter, Rosemary. *Whose News? Politics, the Press and the Third World*. London: Burnett Books, 1978.

Robinson, Gertrude J. "Foreign News Values in the Quebec, English
    Canadian and U.S. Press: A Comparison Study." *Canadian Journal
    of Communication* 9:3 (Summer 1983): 1–32.
Robinson, Gertrude J., and Vernone M. Sparkes. "International News
    in the Canadian and American Press: A Comparative News Flow
    Study." *Gazette* 22:4 (1976): 203–218.
Rogers, Everett, and Francis Balle. *The Media Revolution in America and
    Western Europe.* Norwood, N.J.: Ablex, 1985.
Rosenblum, Mort. *Coups and Earthquakes: Reporting the World for America.*
    New York: Harper and Row, 1979.
Royal Commission on the Press. *Final Report.* London: HMSO, 1977.
Sala-Balust, Ramon. "Journalists' Training: A FIEJ Survey." *FIEJ Bulletin*
    144 (September 30, 1985): 9–12.
Savary, Jean. "Les écoles de journalisme: permis de conduire ou leçon
    de conduite?" *Presse-Actualité* (June-July, 1985): 19.
Schlesinger, Philip. *Putting Reality Together: BBC News.* London: Con-
    stable, 1978.
Schramm, Wilbur. "The State of Communication Research." *Public
    Opinion Quarterly* 23:6 (Spring 1959): 17.
Schudson, Michael. *Discovering the News: A Social History of American
    Newspapers.* New York: Basic Books, 1978.
Semmel, Andrew K. "Foreign News in Four U.S. Elite Dailies: Some
    Comparisons." *Journalism Quarterly* 53:4 (Winter 1976): 732–736.
Shoemaker, Pamela, and Elizabeth Mayfield. "Building a Theory of
    News Content: A Synthesis of Current Approaches." *Journalism
    Monographs* 103, June 1987.
Siebert, Frederick, Theodore Peterson and Wilbur Schramm. *Four The-
    ories of the Press.* Urbana: University of Illinois Press, 1956.
Simpson, D.H. *Commercialization of the Regional Press.* Aldershot: Gower,
    1981.
Simurda, Stephen J. "Can the Stripped-down *Monitor* Stay Afloat?"
    Columbia Journalism Review (March-April 1989): 42–45.
Smith, Anthony. *The British Press Since the War.* Newton Abbot: David
    and Charles, 1974.
———. *The Newspaper: An International History.* London: Thames and
    Hudson, 1979.
———. *The Geopolitics of Information: How Western Culture Dominates the
    World.* New York: Oxford University Press, 1980.
———. *Goodbye Gutenberg: The Newspaper Revolution of the 1980s.* New
    York: Oxford University Press, 1980.
Smith, Gail. "An Analysis of UPI News Flow from Developed and
    Developing Nations to Seven Georgia Newspapers." M.A. The-
    sis, University of Georgia, 1982.

Solomon, Howard M. *Public Welfare, Science and Propaganda in Seventeenth Century France: The Innovations of Théophraste Renaudot*. Princeton, N.J.: Princeton University Press, 1972.

Sreberny-Mohammadi, Annabelle, Kaarle Nordenstreng, Robert Stevenson and Frank Ugboajah. "Foreign News in the Media: International Reporting in 29 Countries." *Reports and Papers on Mass Communication* No. 93. Paris: UNESCO, 1985.

Stempel, Guido H. "Sample Size for Classifying Subject Matter in Dailies." *Journalism Quarterly* 29:2 (Summer 1952): 333–334.

Stevenson, Robert L., and Donald L. Shaw. *Foreign News and the New World Information Order*. Ames: Iowa State University Press, 1984.

Tebbel, John. *The Media in America*. New York: Thomas Y.Crowell, 1974.

Thorn, William J. *Newspaper Circulation: Marketing the News*. New York: Longman, 1987.

Toussaint, Nadine. "La presse quotidienne." *Les Cahiers Français* No. 78 (October-December, 1976).

Tuchman, Gaye. "News, the Newsman's Reality." Ph.D. Dissertation, Brandeis University, 1969.

———. "Objectivity as a Strategic Ritual: An Examination of Newsmen's Notions of Objectivity." *American Journal of Sociology* 77 (January 1972): 660–679.

———. *Making News: A Study in the Construction of Reality*. New York: Free Press, 1978.

Tunstall, Jeremy. *Journalists at Work: Special Correspondents, Their News Organizations, News Sources and Competitor-Colleagues*. London: Constable, 1971.

———. *The Media are American: Anglo-American Media in the World*. London: Constable, 1977.

———. *The Media in Britain*. New York: Columbia University Press, 1983.

UNESCO. *Training for Mass Communication*. Reports and Papers on Mass Communication. Paris: UNESCO, 1975.

Voyenne, Bernard. *Les journalistes français: d'où viennent-ils? Qui sont-ils? Que font-ils?* Paris: Les Editions CFPJ, 1985.

Walker, Martin. *Powers of the Press: Twelve of the World's Influential Newspapers*. New York: Pilgrim Press, 1983.

Waugh, Evelyn. *Scoop*. London: Chapman and Hall, 1938.

Weaver, David H., and G. Cleveland Wilhoit. "Foreign News Coverage in Two U.S. News Services." *Journal of Communication* 31:2 (Spring 1981): 55–63.

———. *The American Journalist: A Portrait of U.S. News People and Their Work*. Bloomington: Indiana University Press, 1986.

————. "A Profile of JMC Educators: Traits, Attitudes and Values." *Journalism Educator* 43:2 (Summer 1988): 4–41.

Weiss, Philip. "Invasion of the Gannettoids." *The New Republic* (February 1, 1987): 18.

What is Taught in Schools of Journalism. University of Missouri Journalism Series Bulletin 54 (1928).

White, David Manning. "The Gate-Keeper: A Case Study in the Selection of News." *Journalism Quarterly* 27:3 (Fall 1950): 383–396.

Whitney, D. Charles. "Mass Communicator Studies: Similarity, Difference and Level of Analysis." In *Individuals in Mass Media Organizations: Creativity and Constraint*, edited by James S. Ettema and D. Charles Whitney, pp. 241–254. Beverly Hills, Calif.: Sage, 1982.

Wilhoit, G. Cleveland, David H. Weaver and Richard G. Gray. "Professional Roles, Values and Ethics of Journalists in Three Democratic Societies." Presented at the Sociology and Social Psychology Section meetings of the 14th Conference and General Assembly of the International Association for Mass Communication Research, Prague, Czechoslovakia, August 27 to September 1, 1984.

Wilhoit, G. Cleveland, and David H. Weaver. "Foreign News Coverage in Two U.S. News Services: An Update." *Journal of Communication* 33:2 (Spring 1983): 132–148.

Williams, Keith. *The English Newspaper: An Illustrated History to 1900*. London: Springfield Books, 1977.

INDEX

About the Author

PHILIP GAUNT is a Visiting Professor in the School of Journalism at Indiana University. He has also been a journalist, a public relations consultant, and a media specialist with UNESCO.